Gracious Spaces

Universal Interiors by Design

Gracious Spaces

Universal Interiors by Design

IRMA LAUFER DOBKIN AND MARY JO PETERSON

McGraw-Hill

New York   San Francisco   Washington, D.C.   Auckland   Bogotá
Caracas   Lisbon   London   Madrid   Mexico City   Milan
Montreal   New Delhi   San Juan   Singapore
Sydney   Tokyo   Toronto

Library of Congress Cataloging-in-Publication Data
Dobkin, Irma.
    Universal interiors by design : gracious spaces / Irma Dobkin,
Mary Jo Peterson.
        p.   cm.
    Includes index.
    ISBN 0-07-017151-3
    1. Universal design.   2. Architecture and the physically
handicapped.   I. Peterson, Mary Jo.   II. Title.
NA2545.P5D63   1999
720'.8—dc21   99-29311
                                                                CIP

McGraw-Hill

A Division of The **McGraw·Hill** Companies

1 2 3 4 5 6 7 8 9 0 DOC/DOC 9 0 4 3 2 1 0 9

ISBN 0-07-017151-3

*The sponsoring editor for this book was Wendy Lochner, the editing supervisor was Caroline
R. Levine, and the production supervisor was Pamela Pelton. This book was set in Giovanni
Book by North Market Street Graphics.*

Printed and bound by R. R. Donnelley & Sons Company.

This book is dedicated to my husband Jim—my mentor, friend, and soulmate, who encouraged me to pursue the journey and was always by my side when the world did not seem to understand. Jim passed away in January 1999 at the age of 58. His boundless capacity to savor life enriched us all and his legacy will be carried on by our children, Jill Sacher and David Dobkin. I cannot help but wonder if Jim had the gift of prophecy. At the conclusion of our chapter he said that even if, as he suspected, he was not to change or age, he would always enjoy and derive satisfaction from our space. The book is also a gift I give myself—the sharing of my journey and my insights with you the reader, in hopes that your home will be your castle, regardless of who you are or what you may become.

Irma Laufer Dobkin

Of the many incredible people who have raised my awareness and my spirit, I dedicate my efforts in this book to the memory of Ron Mace, a teacher to us all and a friend to me.

Mary Jo Peterson

Contents

Foreword   ix

Preface   xi
    Journey Home   xii
    Through the Back Door   xvi
    A Special Thanks   xx

Part One: Background

    CHAPTER 1.   The Move Toward Universal Design   1

    CHAPTER 2.   The Design Process   9

Part Two: Private Homes

    CHAPTER 3.   Aging in Place   15

    CHAPTER 4.   A Vintage Home   27

    CHAPTER 5.   I Lost My Heart in San Francisco   39

    CHAPTER 6.   A Home—A Living Sculpture   47

    CHAPTER 7.   For Both of Us   57

CHAPTER 8.   The Love of Life   67

CHAPTER 9.   Dreams Realized   77

CHAPTER 10.   Mother and Daughter   85

CHAPTER 11.   Synchronicity   95

CHAPTER 12.   On My Own   103

CHAPTER 13.   Freedom of Space and Spirit   115

Part Three: Professionals' Perspective

CHAPTER 14.   Bare Necessities   131

CHAPTER 15.   Real Life Design   141

CHAPTER 16.   On the Street Where You Live   153

CHAPTER 17.   Lifespan Design   161

CHAPTER 18.   For Today, Tomorrow, and Always   167

CHAPTER 19.   The Living Center   175

Products and Sources   185

Manufacturers   193

Index   199

Foreword

THIS IS A BOOK ABOUT CHANGE—CHANGING TIMES, CHANGING ABILITIES, AND CHANGING attitudes. It demonstrates the efforts of two pioneers in the field of universal design as they have recognized the changing needs of people in our evolving society, and how they have adapted their professional lives to address those needs.

This book presents beautiful examples of how we can deal with change in a positive way to meet the physical needs of people as they age and their lives and abilities change. This would be enough to make the book valuable, but the authors have gone beyond examples to show how universal design can be not only functional, but spiritual—spiritual in a sense that enhances the spirit of living and the quality of life. The homes illustrated in this book are inspiring because they show owners and designers how homes can become an extension of the people who live there, enhancing their independence and expanding their choices.

There have been many excellent books published over the last several years about the specific dimensions and relationships between the floors, walls, and fixtures of spaces, but few have addressed the human side in such a compelling way. These two designers have created a book that points a way toward positive change—change in the way that homes are designed so that they enhance the lives of the people who live there, and change in the way designers work to create gracious spaces.

Reading and applying the concepts from this book give us an opportunity to see and understand how all of us can benefit from the Universal Design of Gracious Spaces.

John P. S. Salmen, AIA

John P. S. Salmen, AIA, is the publisher of *Universal Design Newsletter* available at www.UniversalDesign.com and the president of Universal Designers & Consultants, Inc, in Takoma Park, MD.

Preface

Universal Interiors by Design, is about our quality of life as we embark upon the twenty-first century. It is about homes that affirm the human condition from birth to death, and about the triumph of human ingenuity. We must have better, more sensibly designed homes that allow us to fulfill our destiny without barriers; homes that welcome old friends and relatives, that permit a frail parent to visit, so important to families during the holidays. This book is about making homes that are prepared for you no matter what you may be or may become, homes that receive a loved one returning from school, or returning from rehab, without any need for stressful adaptation.

Not only shelter, but retreat and haven, the home must be responsive to a person's needs. With the changing composition of today's households, the challenge for designers, builders, and occupants of homes is to plan a space that not only facilitates basic functions, but renews the spirit. This book responds to that challenge, not with technical information, but with the true stories of imaginative people whose homes succeed in meeting that challenge.

The homes illustrated and explained here truly support the people who live in them. They demonstrate not rules but an approach that embraces and affirms diversity in people. Each design solution reinforces the basic design imperative of first meeting individual needs, seeing and expressing personality in selection of spaces and materials, so that an aesthetic finally emerges. These are predominantly projects of people with particular disabilities who have had the vision and the means to create homes that enhance their quality of life, and do so with a respect for the diversity in abilities and ages of others who will share their space. They run the gamut from high style to laid-back casual and they do so within a variety of budgets.

It is the authors' goal that people will use this book to promote understanding, acceptance, and a positive approach to designing for flexibility and diversity. Individual household members will learn concepts upon which their demands in the marketplace can be based. A fire will be lit under professionals in the design-build industry not just to accept universal design, but to embrace it and expand on it as their creative abilities allow. Homes will celebrate the uniqueness of each client, and will support the variety of people and activities that make up each household.

Journey Home

If I can continue to do today what I did when I was thirty, then I am forever young.

—IRMA LAUFER DOBKIN

When I was in my early forties, an empty-nester embarking on a new life, I began to study interior design. In one of those extraordinary bits of synchronicity that sometimes occur in life, I was entering my studies just as powerful physical and mental changes began to reveal themselves in my mother, Anne Laufer.

This woman, who had always been self-reliant, discovered in her late sixties that her eyesight was failing. She no longer trusted herself behind the wheel and very soon gave up driving. The medical diagnosis followed soon after: macular degeneration. To her shock and ours, she was declared legally blind. She could no longer read, crochet, do needlepoint, play mah-jongg or cards, or take part in any of the activities she so enjoyed. Desperate to help, I urged both my parents to seek assistance and counseling in a support group, but, typical of their generation, they elected to go it alone. Despite my disappointment with their decision, I was nevertheless impressed by my mother's newly emerging skills. Using her hands to supplement her sight, she negotiated around her home and performed her daily chores and rituals. However, as adept as she became in getting around her physical environment, her morale continued to decline. My parents seemed to have come to a tacit agreement whereby my father began to do the things for her that she had once done for herself. Inevitably she forfeited her independence, and bit by bit had to acquiesce to a lesser quality of life.

My mother's travails were only beginning. Within a few months of losing her eyesight, arthritis developed in the form of spinal stenosis, a narrowing or constriction of the backbone. Walking, standing up or sitting down grew increasingly more difficult for her. Next came osteoporosis, a disease which caused a reduction in her bone density, resulting in brittle, fragile bones. A series of sneezes could literally cause several cracked ribs. The final blow was Alzheimer's disease, the slow deterioration of her mental capacities that showed itself about the same time my father was diagnosed with leukemia. Does this sound like the Book of Job? I was beginning to realize that for some, the aging process is a nightmare from which they cannot awaken.

In less than three years my mother went from being an able-bodied, self-reliant woman to a blind, dependent wheelchair user. In her small Florida apartment she still managed fairly well, but when she visited our wonderful and spacious Maryland home, not only was she challenged, but she also was unintentionally demeaned. A small step here, another up or down there, meant she had to call for assistance. These seemingly small barriers totally compromised her independence. Just about everything in our home, including my sumptuously padded stylish furniture, made her aware that she was an invalid.

As awful as it may sound, the truth is that at first I was defensive about our home and its furnishings. "Why couldn't she try harder?" I wondered. Did she want me to change my home into a nursing facility?

I have since realized that I was simply in denial about her needs, about adjusting to them. I guess I wanted my mother to stay as she had always been— there for me. I wanted the clock to stand still, but of course it does not, and having to feel guilty every time my parents visited was not adding quality to our relationship at a time when my parents most needed our support. I could no longer deny the difficulties she encountered in my home.

About this time in design school I was learning about *programming*—weighing a client's needs and wants. I was examining what activities had to be conducted in a home, what rooms or spaces would be required to serve those needs and desires, what furnishings and equipment were necessary to support those activities, and so on. As my knowledge grew, it was natural for me to begin to evaluate my own home. To my surprise, the very first deficit uncovered was the Italian modular seating in my living room. With a 42-in depth, a seat height of 14 in, and a sloping back, standing after sitting presented a Procrustean task. My mother was not being unreasonable. It was the furniture design that was!

Concurrent with my discovery of the sofa problems, I was given a class project to design a barrier-free home. Given dozens of personal and spatial requirements to incorporate in the design, I began reading about *anthropometrics* (measuring the human body to determine differences in individuals and groups) and *ergonomics* (the relationship between human physiology and the physical environment). General literature on problems faced by the handicapped was also assigned. Needless to say, these assignments were exceptionally relevant to my own situation, and I pored over the learning materials alert to every detail and suggestion.

I set about designing a project home that would permit a disabled person to function as an active and independent family member. Behind every design decision lay thoughts of my mother, who could have so benefited from these carefully planned spaces, open areas aggregated on a single level. Research into home products proved a real eye-opener. I couldn't find any kitchen or bathroom cabinets manufactured specifically for wheelchair users! Everything I wanted to incorporate would have to be jury-rigged to allow access by a seated user.

I also discovered that safety products offered few aesthetic choices. Let me be more direct: unless cafeteria or dormitory style was to become the next American design rage, the homes of handicapped people were doomed to be ugly. There simply were no aesthetic choices.

I began to realize that no matter how much creativity I poured into my design for a truly accessible home made in durable and safe materials, the end result would still end up looking sadly institutional. This simply wasn't good enough. My own parents had instilled in me that our home is our castle, or should be.

Homes that do not take into account the changing skills and abilities we experience as we pass through life do not enrich us; they diminish us and weaken our self-esteem. I saw very clearly that we must have homes that enable, even as the occupants become less able.

America is a relatively young country. Being an American is almost synonymous with ability, with our undaunted can-do spirit. We have little robots that send pictures from the surface of Mars back to Earth. We have micromachines and microengines the size of a grain of pollen. Being an American means believing you can do anything you set your mind to. So why is it that when tasks once easy for us become more difficult with age or infirmity, we blame ourselves for being less than we should be?

I want to share with you just how far a situation can go before we demand the environmental changes we really need. Several years ago I was asked to meet with a vigorous couple in their eighties. They were considering remodeling a home in which they had lived for 50 years. As a young boy, the husband had had polio. There were no signs of the damage done until he was well into his seventies, when the more affected leg began to drag. He began using a cane for walking and for getting up and down. Time passed, and two canes were needed, then a walker, and finally a scooter when his legs would no longer respond. By then the husband was 80 years old.

The scooter became part of their home, so their home had to change appreciably. The scooter needed more room than legs had required, so the wife lined and stacked all the living room furniture along a wall, making room for the scooter but ending the room's usefulness as a living room. It was just a circulation space which stored furniture. Was this aesthetically pleasing? Absolutely not. It was sad and it was demoralizing. But the couple was forced into other adaptations that were even worse.

The house had a narrow hall leading to bedrooms and bath. The scooter, guided by the driver's great maneuverability skills, could get to the master bedroom. Once there, however, there was no room for the scooter to turn. The effect of this was that use of the bathroom was impossible, and he was forced to use a hall bathroom. The door was not wide enough. How did he handle this bathroom access barrier? He slid down from his scooter seat and crawled into the bathroom as he had crawled when ducking gunfire as a soldier in the European Theater, dragging his legs by propelling forward with arms and elbows. Once in the bathroom, he maneuvered his 6-ft body up by bracing on the side of the tub and then heaving his body onto the toilet.

It was not until several months later, during a doctor's appointment, that he and his wife finally saw how unacceptable this can-do fix was. Bruises along his shins alerted the doctor that more was at work than just the polio. When the doctor heard how the bruises and skin burns had occurred, he immediately contacted an occupational therapist to help the couple devise a better solution. Who knows how much longer this man might have endured discomfort and indignity if his doctor had not interceded?

Many of us know of elderly, frail people who have stopped bathing because they fear falling in the shower or tub. We know of others who become prisoners in their own homes because they cannot negotiate steps. Very determined people often devise adaptive coping strategies like the one I just described, but doesn't it make you angry that people have to be demeaned and endangered because homes are designed as if the occupants were Peter Pan and would stay young forever? I know it incenses me, and I want to raise the public's awareness that we are changing creatures who require adaptive environments as we age.

Through the Back Door

If you only look at what is, you might never attain what could be.

—MARY JO PETERSON

Aha!

At a point in my career and life in general when I was asking if I could hope to make a difference in the world, I turned the focus of my kitchen and bath design work to people with disabilities. A past client, now a friend and advisor, encouraged me to put my love of people and of creating these two types of spaces together. It was my grand scheme that I would work with each client as I had been, establishing the needs and parameters of the project, and creating a kitchen or bathroom that more than accomplished the goals. The difference would be that the client's needs would be nontraditional. The design team would include medical advisors, and the results would be not only beautiful and new, but newly open to the client.

One of my first projects was a bath remodel. The goal was to enable the client to transfer independently and to do so into a tub, rather than a shower. The day the job was complete, I received a call from the client thanking me and telling me that she was celebrating her first bath in 15 years. I was hooked. Most of us have to make a living, but not all of us can have the joy in work that I have found.

While my clients with disabilities were growing in numbers, I continued to work with builders, architects, and referrals from previous clients. I learned that much was possible using the same lovely parts and pieces that had always been a part of the package, but they had to be used in nontraditional ways. I learned that many of the things I designed to support or give access to a client with a disability would also improve the space for an able-bodied client. In fact, I learned that the question to ask clients was what they wanted of a new space, not based on what they already knew a kitchen or bath could do, but on what they wished it could do. Aha! My focus needed not be people with disabilities to the exclusion of others, but could be improved flexibility and access for all clients. What a concept! Of course, that concept is universal design, and so I entered, through the back door, into the world of believers in universal design.

This *Aha!* experience is part of the reason for *Gracious Spaces*. Over and over, we discover new benefits to some of the nontraditional solutions that a unique need for access demands. This book is the story of homes created through this discovery process, the plans and changes, and the teams who created them.

In working toward the ideal of universal design, there are several lessons that keep being repeated. They involve listening skills, team work, and cooperation.

Listening

Having always believed myself to be a good listener, every day I am learning new dimensions of listening. The trick seems to be to listen from beginning to end, not hearing the first sentence and assuming the rest. Again, it was an experience with a client that drew my attention to my listening skills.

For this incredible woman who was rebuilding her life, this time with no use of her legs and little use of her arms, I felt great respect and the strong desire to give her independence and strengthen her dignity. Initial master suite plans included a closet that was an engineering feat, allowing her to see and select her daily attire. When she made no remark about the closet, I asked. She told me that dressing herself would take so much of her time that it was not of interest to her. By letting someone else dress her, she gained several hours each day for the things that mattered to her. Had I been listening instead of projecting my desires for her, I would have heard that the first time.

Because we each see things through different eyes, with disability or without, we can learn more each time we work through the design process with a client. *Gracious Spaces* attempts to offer that experience as told by the teams that created the projects in the book.

The Team

When I began my transformation into specializing in universal design, I needed a variety of professionals for support, and I discovered a number of wise and talented people who were way ahead of me. The group was diverse—health professionals, designers of products and spaces, government housing authorities and social agency workers, researchers and educators, advocates for people of varying ages and ability, and end users with specific needs. Each team member truly had something to offer and something to learn. Today, the makeup of the group is the same, but it has grown exponentially. The diversity of this group creates the dynamics for the best of professional teamwork, and whenever time and money permit, that's what is happening.

An example of the generous spirit in the universal design community, Ron Mace may not have known everything on the subject, but he came closer than anyone that I have met. When, as a total novice, I presumed to call him, he spoke to me at length. I had been warned that he would be hard to reach and not to be disappointed when I did not connect. The opposite occurred. We connected in such a way as to support my learning, my work, and my spirit for as long as I knew him. It was not until some time after our first telephone conversation that

I met Ron and learned of his disabilities. I know we are not to make heroes out of people with disabilities, but Ron was a hero for me first, and a person with a disability much later.

This sharing of knowledge, information, and experience is another piece of what makes universal design work. It is a great team and each person seems eager to help the next.

Then and Now

For those involved in the universal design movement for many years, progress may seem slow, but in the time I've been working at it, things have changed dramatically.

Five years ago, people would ask me, "What is universal design?" and when it was explained, they would pat me on the head and say, "That's sweet dear," and dismiss it to get back to the real world. Today, there are still a few of those responses, but it is more common for a worthwhile conversation to take place regarding flexibility for the variety of household members using a kitchen or bath, or design to support our aging process.

Changes have occurred in part due to passage of access codes and guidelines. While most of the laws and codes deal with commercial spaces or multihousing only, awareness has been raised. We are flooded with statistics about the aging of America. Whether seen as good news or bad, behind this growing awareness is the sobering fact that our market is changing, and we have to design and build responsively or lose market share. The amazing is happening. "Handicapped accessibility" brought negative responses, no matter how attractive or how functional. Today universal design is gradually gaining positive support as the state of the art or simply as good design.

The Future

We still have such a long way to go, but we are building momentum. Whether as an ideal to work toward or as an attainable goal, universal design is gaining attention. It should be our objective that one day every designer of spaces or products will consider universal design principles just as integrally as the other elements and principles of design. We will no longer need a name—we will simply acknowledge as quality only those creations that respect the diversity in people.

A Special Thanks...

For generosity and patience in sharing their homes and their journeys, the authors thank the homeowners and designers of the spaces and stories told in this book.

For financial contributions toward the photography and drawings, the authors thank the Kohler Company, General Electric Appliances, and the International Furnishings and Design Association Education Foundation.

The authors also thank the many friends and professionals who have contributed to the content and the preparation of this book, especially

- Annette DePaepe, CKD, CBD, ASID—drafting

- Mary Seymour—typing and formatting

- Steven Winter Associates—support and content

- Bill Lebovitch—special photography

Part One
Background

Chapter 1

The Move Toward Universal Design

IN RESPONSE TO CHANGING LIFESTYLES AND A GROWING APPRECIATION FOR DIVERSITY in people, we are moving toward environments that support and adapt to a variety of people. In the homes we design, build, and furnish, we must create spaces that incorporate flexibility and adaptability, allowing for use by most people most of the time. This growing trend is toward universal design which, once incorporated, will be simply good design.

Historically, the built environment has been designed for the nonelderly able-bodied adult male. Since that description fits less than 8 percent of our population, the result is environments which create handicaps or barriers for the rest of us. Demographics, legislation, public awareness, and personal experience are pressing us to examine the basic assumptions we have used in design, and sometimes to replace them with what we learn when we listen to the people we are designing for. The result is an expanding interest in design that breaks traditional molds and, with those molds, many of the barriers we have adjusted to in the past. Instead, we can strive to create environments, and particularly homes that embrace the diversity in household makeup.

A Brief History of Public Standards

The American National Standards Institute published the first design standard on accessibility, Specifications for Making Buildings and Facilities Accessible to and Usable by the Physically Handicapped (ANSI 117.1-1961). Since then, awareness of the need for accessibility has grown. Recognition of the rights of minorities, including children, the disabled, and the elderly, has grown as well.

The Uniform Federal Accessibility Standard (UFAS), used for all federally funded construction, incorporated much of the ANSI standard, improving uniformity. In 1988, the Fair Housing Amendment to the Civil Rights Act of 1968 was passed into law, with access guidelines impacting multiple housing units. In 1990, the Americans with Disabilities Act (ADA) was passed, with guidelines first passed in 1991, stipulating mandatory conditions for public spaces, and truly changing the way we view the built environment.

The intent of these regulations and the building codes and guidelines that have grown out of them is not "separate but equal." It is inclusive design for use by as broad a population as possible. These regulations undergo repeated review and revision to clarify and to increase consistency. While at times the guidelines can seem restrictive, they have gone far to raise our awareness and provide guidance.

Changing Lifestyles

In terms of lifestyle, from post–World War II to the present, we have become a country where everyone shares in the responsibilities and activities of home life. Home has become the hub of family and social activities. Time is scarce and time together even more so. Where once a task was performed by one person, today it may be done by anyone in the household, and often by more than one person at the same time.

The impact of these changes is felt throughout the home, and particularly in high-function areas. For example, in kitchen and bath spaces, flexibility, adaptability, and access for a variety of activities performed by a variety of household members is imperative. The same bathroom may be a workout room for a mom in the morning, a quick shower for dad in the evening, and a soak in the tub for a child or a grandma before bed. The kitchen might find Junior cooking dinner while Gram and Sis bake cookies, with Mom paying bills while Dad does laundry.

Further changes in the needs of households center around independence for people with disabilities. The largest segment of people with disabilities is the group with impaired mobility or dexterity (whether injury- or illness-related). "This group includes 9,517,000 Americans who use mobility aids, from crutches and walking sticks to wheelchairs and scooters. It also includes 24 million people with arthritis, 18 million of whom are under the age of 65. An estimated 8 million Americans have significant visual impairments and over 22 million have hearing impairments" (based on National Center for Health Statistics, 1994). The number of people with disabilities is growing. People born with a disability or having injury- or illness-related disabilities are surviving at a greater rate. Life expectancies are longer, especially for women.

A major force in the changing needs of households is the aging process. By the year 2020, over 20 percent of our population will be over 65. According to an American Association of Retired Persons (AARP) survey, 84 percent of people in this age group wish to stay in their homes and *age in place.* Exploration of residential design options relating to independent and assisted living is part of the national health care reform movement. These statistics become more real as we reflect on our own lifestyles and circumstances.

We can think of parents or grandparents who have moved out of their homes, perhaps into ours or into a group setting. We want to see them leading independent and dignified lives. We can recognize the roles of those elders and children in our daily household responsibilities. We can acknowledge the difficult or impossible barriers in our homes that become apparent only when we experience physical disabilities. Best of all, we can create homes that are beautiful and flexible and allow for these differences in the lives of our home communities.

Toward the goal of making every space and product we create universal, the following principles were developed under the direction of the Center for Universal Design. While every guideline may not be relevant to all designs, these principles provide a measure for each space that is planned or each product that is specified. They are as follows:

PRINCIPLE ONE: EQUITABLE USE

The design is useful and marketable to any group of users.

Guidelines:

1a. Provide the same means of use for all users: identical whenever possible; equivalent when not.

1b. Avoid segregating or stigmatizing any users.

1c. Provisions for privacy, security, and safety should be equally available to all users.

PRINCIPLE TWO: FLEXIBILITY IN USE

The design accommodates a wide range of individual preferences and abilities.

Guidelines:

2a. Provide choice in methods of use.

2b. Accommodate right- or left-handed access and use.

2c. Facilitate the user's accuracy and precision.

2d. Provide adaptability to the user's pace.

PRINCIPLE THREE: SIMPLE AND INTUITIVE USE

Use of the design is easy to understand, regardless of the user's experience, knowledge, language skills, or current concentration level.

Guidelines:

3a. Eliminate unnecessary complexity.

3b. Be consistent with user expectations and intuition.

3c. Accommodate a wide range of literacy and language skills.

3d. Arrange information consistent with its importance.

3e. Provide effective prompting for sequential actions.

3f. Provide timely feedback during and after task completion.

PRINCIPLE FOUR: PERCEPTIBLE INFORMATION

The design communicates necessary information effectively to the user, regardless of ambient conditions or the user's sensory abilities.

Guidelines:

4a. Use different modes (pictorial, verbal, tactile) for redundant presentation of essential information.

4b. Provide adequate contrast between essential information and its surroundings.

4c. Maximize "legibility" of essential information in all sensory modalities.

4d. Differentiate elements in ways that can be described (i.e., make it easy to give instructions or directions).

4e. Provide compatibility with a variety of techniques or devices used by people with sensory limitations.

PRINCIPLE FIVE: TOLERANCE FOR ERROR

The design minimizes hazards and the adverse consequences of accidental or unintended actions.

Guidelines:

5a. Arrange elements to minimize hazards and errors: most used elements, most accessible; hazardous elements eliminated, isolated, or shielded.

5b. Provide warnings of hazards and errors.

5c. Provide fail safe features.

5d. Discourage unconscious action in tasks that require vigilance.

PRINCIPLE SIX: LOW PHYSICAL EFFORT

The design can be used efficiently and comfortably and with a minimum of fatigue.

Guidelines:

6a. Allow user to maintain a neutral body position.

6b. Use reasonable operating forces.

6c. Minimize repetitive actions.

6d. Minimize sustained physical effort.

PRINCIPLE SEVEN: SIZE AND SPACE FOR APPROACH AND USE

Appropriate size and space is provided for approach, reach, manipulation, and use regardless of user's body size, posture, or mobility.

Guidelines:

7a. Provide a clear line of sight to important elements for any seated or standing user.

7b. Make reach to all components comfortable for any seated or standing user.

7c. Accommodate variations in hand and grip size.

7d. Provide adequate space for the use of assistive devices or personal assistance.

It must be acknowledged that the principles of universal design in no way comprise all criteria for good design, only universally usable design. Certainly, other factors are important, such as aesthetics, cost, safety, gender and cultural appropriateness, and these aspects should be taken into consideration as well when designing.

SOURCE: The Principles of Universal Design, Version 1.1—12/7/95, The Center for Universal Design, North Carolina State University. Major funding provided by the National Institute on Disability and Rehabilitation Research, Copyright © 1995 North Carolina State University.

Chapter 2

The Design Process

THE CONCEPT OF PROGRAMMING A DESIGN IS THE FOUNDATION OF GOOD DESIGN. AN assessment or survey establishes user needs and the parameters of the project. These requirements become the barometer by which a designer or homeowner evaluates the suitability of a design for a specific use or users. The program also drives the creative process. It captures not only what the space must do but the spirit of the space, its ambiance. No matter how dramatic, beautiful, or exciting it may be, if the user's needs are not satisfied the space will not succeed. Function and ambiance should work in concert toward a unified and logical overall design.

In designing a space to meet specific needs, the following items should be considered during the design process:

1. Who will use the space?

2. What are the user's needs?

3. Where is the space, and how much of it is being impacted?

4. How will the space be used?

5. What furniture and equipment are needed to perform the intended activities?

6. What will the overall style be? The feel? What will it say to and about the people who use it (ambiance and image)?

The Process

Sometimes the answers to these questions need to be very specific, particularly in high-function areas like the kitchen or the bathroom. These are spaces where a person will perform tasks beyond simply entering and occupying the space. In designing for these spaces, design professionals frequently use extensive surveys to establish desired outcomes. Examples are available in Mary Jo Peterson, *Universal Kitchen and Bathroom Planning* (National Kitchen and Bath Association, Hackettstown, N.J., 1996).

Sometimes these answers are elusive. A design professional and a client must work together until the program is clearly defined. The result of this investment will be a design that truly satisfies the clients' needs.

Historically, designers of products, furnishings, and even the spaces of our homes have not always attended to the human condition and its intrinsic variables. Design has been focused on appearance, sometimes to the exclusion of function, or it has been focused on the rare "average person." Economics of volume, critical to mass production, and tradition have created products that force people to adapt, rather than products that adapt to the users. Following are several examples to provoke thinking and the application of universal design principles in the programming of a design.

Check Out Your Chairs

It often seems that home furnishings disregard the human condition. Furniture trends of the past few years include sumptuously oversized upholstered sofas and chairs, sinfully soft and larger than life and often adorned with mounds of down pillows. It is very difficult for most people to get out of these overstuffed styles, as they are too deep and too low. Check out your chairs—are they really as comfortable and efficient as they could be?

More likely, the connection between furniture, designed spaces, and the reality of how the human body works is missing. While not deliberate, this oversight signifies an omission and a lack of understanding.

Design professionals need to incorporate the diversity of human abilities when creating spaces or products. *Ergonomics*, the study of the relationship between human physiology and the physical environment, examines how humans interact with physical objects like chairs, control panels, desks, and the like. This is as basic as programming for good design. Ergonomics measures everything—the distance above an arm can reach from a seated position; the amount of clear, unobstructed space required for a person to pass through the space without knocking into partitions; other people or objects in the environment. These considerations become even more critical in high-function areas like the kitchen and the bath.

In the workplace, the study of ergonomics has had great impact. Here, the chair has received primary attention. We have adjustability, crucial for comfort, health, and safety. Today's modern office chair has countless anatomically induced criteria that guide its design and construction.

The application of ergonomic studies has not been as apparent in home furnishings. As consumers, we have historically had few choices. If enough of us demanded ergonomically designed home furnishings, eventually we would get them.

The Throne Room

Bathroom design is a crucial element for any comfortable home. While some aspects of the design of fixtures and the space they occupy have changed, in many ways they have not.

Designs of lavatories for today's bathrooms leave no reason for anyone to create less than a beautiful and supportive sink area. Options for shower design are also limitless, and designers are moving toward comfort and safety in the shower environments. Probably the only thing standing in the way of design progress in these areas is *tradition*. Old habits die hard, so the concept of no threshold in a shower or a wall-hung vanity with adjacent storage rather than the traditional vanity cabinet is at first hard to accept. As more spaces are created with universal planning, they will become the tradition, and the improvement in function will be more fully embraced.

Although the toilet is a little slower to change, there are options in toilet height today. *Flexibility* in height would be the ideal. The adjustable-height toilet remains in the prototype phase, and is not available to most of us.

Bathtubs—again, slow to change—are challenging for even the most able-bodied to enter and exit. Depth and the occasional addition of a stepped approach can create unsafe situations. A deck to sit on for transfer and a rail or grab bar are possible solutions, and good design can incorporate these elements into the lines of a bathroom so they enhance the attractiveness of the design.

Builders, Developers, and the Design Process

Boyce Thompson, noted editor of *Builder Magazine,* in an editorial on future home building in America (December 1997), said, "Most new homes today dictate rather than accommodate lifestyles." Everywhere we read about lifestyle-generated design; growing numbers of builders are turning to area-specific designers to respond to this trend; and yet change is slow. Application of a universal design program, with inherent flexibility and improved access, might greatly assist in the evolution of the homes we build.

How will we ensure reasonable and responsive design of homes and home furnishings? Education is the only way. Consumers must demand attributes that will truly make our homes suitable to our lifestyles. Designers of products and spaces and builders must support these demands. Hopefully, *Gracious Spaces* will help promote an understanding that the home can be both beautiful and beneficial, and can accommodate us as we change with the passage of time.

Part Two

Private Homes

In this section, homeowners share their experiences in creating homes that are both supportive and full of personality. These projects have been visited by the authors and the stories are as written by the homeowners or as told to the authors. Whether expensive or economical, each of these homes is both gracious and universal, offering ideas and inspiration for anyone exploring home design.

Chapter 3

Aging in Place

HOMEOWNER: **Jim and Irma**
DESIGNER: **Irma Laufer Dobkin**
PHOTOGRAPHER: **Gordon Beall**

OUR HOME IS A SPRAWLING QUASI-RAMBLER WITH SMALL INCREMENTAL LEVEL CHANGES throughout. For years I found myself frustrated by the existing master bedroom, but I was reluctant to simply redecorate. When I sat down and analyzed what about it was wrong—the circulation, the improperly scaled furniture and fixtures, the lack of privacy, the unsafe conditions, the poor lighting, and so on— we determined it was time to make a change.

Background

So much self-esteem comes from being independent—capable of taking care of oneself. Among the original bedroom's greatest deficiencies were the barriers in the environment. They, as much as the physical changes in our bodies, would have prevented us from continuing to do simple daily tasks by ourselves. The list was long: doors awkwardly interfering with circulation spaces, a bed that was far too low, a sunken tub that had no railing to hold while stepping in and out, lighting that could not be operated from bed, inadequate general lighting, a toi-

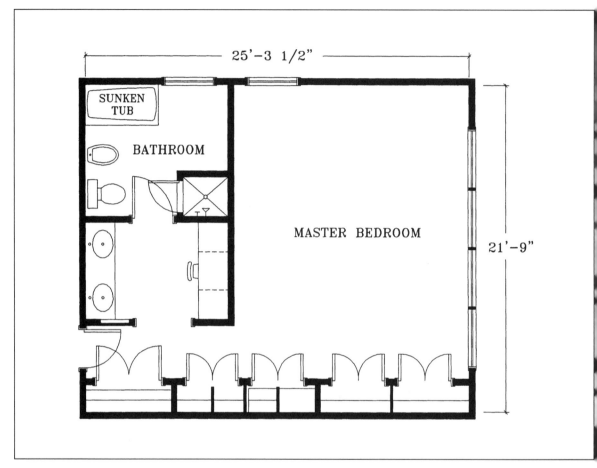

Figure 3-1   Irma and Jim: Before floor plan.

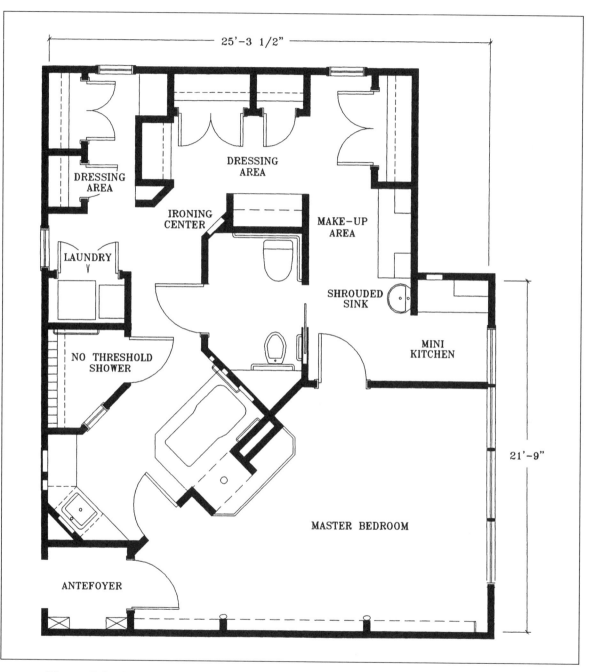

Figure 3-2   Irma and Jim: After floor plan showing compartmentalized activity areas, elimination of congestion, segregation of noise and light, storage at point of use, enlarged door openings, and addition of laundry.

let that was too low, and a shower with a curb and no grab bars. All these impediments were substantial existing barriers that would have prevented Jim and me from safely or graciously growing older in the master bedroom, even without physical disability.

The Challenge

In considering improvements for the new bedroom, we became aware of serious shortcomings in the old design. In the first rendition of the bedroom, the most prominent features were the view of the woods and the art on the walls. Furniture was kept to a minimum. We had a platform bed that measured 14 in from floor to mattress top, which did not become challenging until I began getting out of bed several times a night.

The long corridor entry to the bedroom had many doors that interfered with both the operation of closet areas and entry into the space itself. The sink and makeup area had no doors. Without doors to contain them, sound and light became problematic when my husband's wake-up time and mine no longer coincided. Placing a headboard against a shared wet wall as we had done compounded the noise problem. We had wanted a dramatic bath in the original bedroom, but the sunken whirlpool became a hazard as I began to make regular sleepy excursions to the toilet during the night.

Lighting was planned to accent art and for specific tasks, but general lighting had been overlooked, creating visual confusion. I require abundant lighting, especially for grooming activities. Not only does light help in distinguishing between similar colors and shades, it discloses subtle flaws and blemishes that I would rather find myself.

The split-level nature of our home made it especially important that the bedroom suite be self-contained. There were other, idiosyncratic, requirements too. Coffee upon awakening seemed like Nirvana to me. Thus, a minikitchen in the new bedroom suite became an indispensable feature.

As Virgos we like everything compartmentalized, hence the suite's configuration. There would be places to sleep, to read, to watch television; others for bathing and toileting; and individualized dressing areas. Task-specific items would be stored within those areas so we could retrieve them with minimal effort.

To preserve independence and self-sufficiency, the new bedroom had to be universally designed, which meant:

- Wheelchair accessibility

- Curbless shower

- Wide doorways and unobstructed circulation routes

- Grab bars wherever needed

Lever handles on doors and faucets could eliminate a potential barrier, especially for someone who anticipated increasing immobility and strength loss due to arthritis.

Process and Solutions

We continued to refine our needs. Our private rituals were different. To avoid conflict we wanted separate grooming areas. By placing Jim's dressing area a distance from the sleep area he would be more comfortable getting ready at 5:30 in the morning without disturbing me. We were willing to sacrifice view to assure greater peace of mind by having the bed face the room's entry.

When the assessment was complete, we moved to the next stage, developing a fundamental concept that would guide the evaluation of proposed solutions. What emerged initially surprised me. Not only was accessibility critical, but to meet our needs the space had to be romantic in a most fundamental sense— exciting and beautiful. Maybe growing older isn't that frightening after all.

We hoped to preserve the existing architecture and match materials used in the first bedroom. The wall facing the rear yard was of fixed glass panels, dictating the size of the sleeping area. A diagonal wall borrowed space from the sleep area to increase the grooming area. With the toilet centrally located, all other areas were designed around it.

The minikitchen would be adjacent to the sleep area. I could almost sleepwalk to my coffee every morning. Included in this space was an undercounter refrigerator, an automatic icemaker, a microwave, a wet bar, and an instant hot water dispenser.

The sleep area was kept relatively small. It was made as big as was needed for the activities that would go on here, namely sleeping and watching television in bed. The adjustable bed was Jim's idea. Independent controls would allow each of us to adjust the head and foot positions or the massage mechanism. The two twin beds were treated as an oversized queen bed with a custom fully uphol-stered headboard. I designed custom night tables that would house the controls and their heavy wiring in a tilt-down drawer. The fixed nightstands would house the controls for the bed, the window treatment, reading and bath lighting, and the television.

I planned a fixed bureau that would house the bedding—again, the purpose was to keep materials and equipment close to a routinely performed activity. I wanted to ensure that our furniture would not move when leaned upon. The storage bureau, in fact, looked like a raised hearth, so why not a fireplace? A fireplace in a bedroom was certainly romantic, so in it went. I shifted the fire-box to the left to enhance our view of it from the bed. That left a niche for a tele-vision. Never having had a television in our bedroom, I initially resisted. Upon reconsideration, however, the television fit the concept of a self-contained liv-ing environment.

Next came the layout for the main bathing area and Jim's grooming area. The largest fixture was the bathtub. An accessible approach to the tub and a seated transfer area dictated the length of the diagonal wall. The final configuration of the space required many attempts before all the pieces of this spatial mosaic fit. The shower was a separate challenge. It had to be large to accommodate a wheelchair, a walker, or an assistant if ever things came to that. It had to be placed in a wide and deep space. Such an area was available beyond Jim's vanity. It was important that the access routes within the bathroom have parallel walls to help signal logi-cal wayfinding. Therefore, the shower was designed with an angled wall.

That angled wall would confront anyone entering the bathroom. A beveled glass insert minimized the monumentality of the soaring angled partition. Despite the height and directional changes of that wall, the beauty of the glass held the focal point.

The design of the curbless shower was my greatest challenge. In order to maintain the large floor tiles that I wanted to use, a corrugated solid surface trough was created, beneath which was a regular shower drain for water management. The entire shower floor was sloped. The slope was held to an almost imperceptible differential that was still sufficient to shunt the water within the shower toward the trough. It worked perfectly.

The custom safety glass door with a rubber stopper at the bottom made this an airtight environment with the steam unit on. Oversized door pulls worked well. The 20-in-deep bench and the oversized shower itself would permit a portable wheelchair to come into the space. The grab bars would facilitate transfer, and a chair could fold and lean against the beveled glass partition. Temperature controls could be preset to avoid scalding. A fixed showerhead and an adjustable hand-held shower would permit a full variety of bathing positions. Corner chrome shelves at different heights would permit access for seated or standing bathers.

The size of the toilet area was guided by the circulation widths I wished to maintain throughout the space and by the requirement for wheelchair transfer. To avoid the sequestered feeling that is so common, a large skylight was installed. For privacy, a pocket door consisting of an exterior solid core door on a heavy-duty ceiling track was used. With a bumper in the pocket of the recess, a gentle tap of an elbow would set the door in motion. This is actually the hub of the entire space.

The toilet and bidet that we already had were in perfect condition. Since they were low and sleek, a Corian platform that matched the outline of the bases was fabricated, raising the seats to about 16½″ above finished floor (AFF). Previously they had been about 14¼″ AFF—too low for tall users and very tough on the lower back and knees. Grab bars were installed to surround both for safety. A portable chest was used to house extra rolls of toilet paper and other on-site necessities. Recessed fluorescents added a soft glow and are fabulous because they have a life expectancy of nearly 8 years. Dramatic crystal sconces were placed on the rise of the skylight above. Although an interior stall, the out-of-doors is right there.

The laundry center shared a wet wall with the shower, placing it in Jim's dressing area. He, of course, being in his midfifties and not part of the liberated generation, has no idea how to do laundry, but it was also conveniently located for my use. There was an angled partition in that area that had no purpose. Accordingly, I put a recessed ironing board in that wall. It made wonderful sense. Where else does one discover creased clothing other than taking it off or putting it on?

The size and number of mirrored doors I planned to reuse from the original bedroom established the size and location of the closets. Space allocation was based upon how much we each had to hang and to store in drawers or on shelves. Jim rejected what was originally planned as a walk-in closet for him. He did not want to dress inside a closet. In that one instance we sacrificed accessibility for "real" closets.

I wanted to have a designated place for garment bags and suitcases that would not interfere with our regular routines when they were out for packing. In several areas we installed retractable garment hangers, which worked well.

Although we were creating a luxury space on a generous budget, there were economies. The cost of labor to bring the wiring up through the floor to reach the night tables was the same that it would have been to locate it anywhere. The point is to try to think of all the accouterments you want and plan for them initially rather than as an afterthought. *Planned* is more affordable and certainly less disruptive to the construction schedule. Many of the objects that I already had could be reused as mentioned—the toilet, bidet, whirlpool, mirrored closet doors, and many custom cabinets. Recycling of that type is kind to both environment and pocketbook.

Aha!

Several months after we were settled into our new bedroom, Jim declared that even if, as he suspected, he did not change or age, he would always enjoy and derive satisfaction from the space. Our master suite may not be perfect, but it comes pretty close. It is affirming, efficient, glamorous, and a wonderful way to start and end the day. It is a joy to use. We anticipate that it will support our changes as we age in place. And it is romantic.

Figure 3-3 Irma and Jim: Ironing board and laundry; includes automatic shutoff.

Figure 3-4 Irma and Jim: Curbless shower includes 13-by-13-in nonskid tiles sloped toward trough-style drain, safety-glass door, antiscald valve, varied height storage, and grab bars, and uses all universal fixtures.

Figure 3-5 Irma and Jim: Minikitchen showing fixed window that can become future egress route.

Chapter 4

A Vintage Home

HOMEOWNERS: Juliet and Marc
DESIGNER: Mary Jo Peterson
ARCHITECT: David Polk
PHOTOGRAPHER: John Bessler

PART OF PHILADELPHIA'S HISTORY, THIS HOME WAS BUILT IN 1903 AS THE CARRIAGE house and heating plant for a 75-room mansion, designed by Boston architects Peabody and Stearns. It survived the destruction of the mansion in 1939 and the breakup of the 571-acre estate, becoming a gardener's cottage and greenhouse and, for the last 50 years, a residence. It was not until its present owners moved in that it became accessible as well.

Background

At the time of her injury, Juliet lived in and loved her home, a true Cotswald-style cottage built in 1923. With multiple levels and narrow doors and passageways, it was a nonaccessible space. While still in the hospital, she was told that the changes required to provide her access in this space would be significant, distorting, and virtually impossible. Serendipitously, a friend told her that a one-level Arts and Crafts–style house was on the market that might interest her. Juliet moved fast. With a 1-hour visit on a day pass from the hospital, Juliet and her

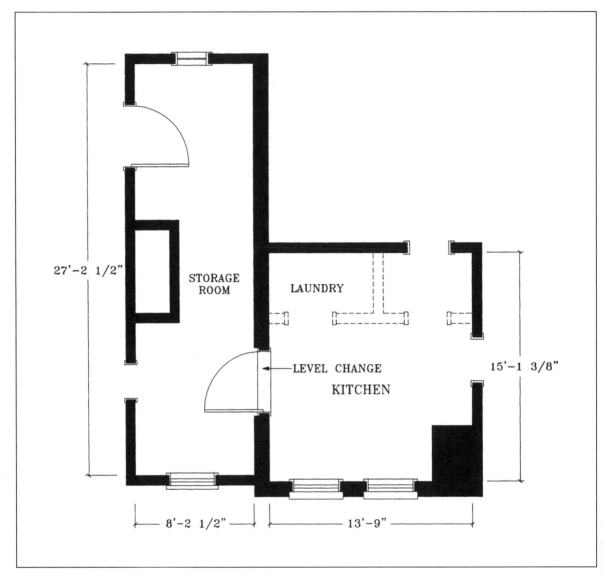

Figure 4-1   Juliet and Marc: Before floor plan.

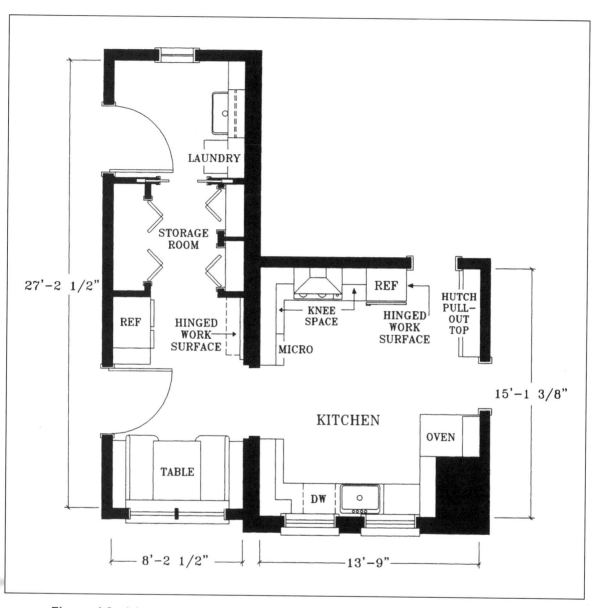

Figure 4-2 Juliet and Marc: The new space, showing elimination of congestion, reassigned activity areas, and improved storage, access, and workflow.

husband Marc bought what is now their home. Leaving the hospital to enter a new home, Juliet also entered a new phase of her life, this time using a wheel-chair.

The Challenge

Although Juliet doesn't say it, the international travel that is part of her work drives home the lack of consideration or respect for a person using a wheelchair in the built environment. To counter this frustration, the need for home to be truly supportive, truly a haven, is even greater.

On moving into their new home, Juliet and Marc only had to adjust thresholds and renovate their master bath to suit their taste and their needs. One year later, they added a pool wing for Juliet's exercise routine and expanded the front entry to improve both its function and its appearance. Five years later, it was time to look to the kitchen, having saved the best, or the worst, for last.

As a professional couple, weekday cooking essentially involved thawing and reheating their housekeeper's fare in the microwave. In the future they hoped to enjoy cooking together and to do more entertaining, truly a feat of magic in their existing kitchen. Unique to this household, cooking was not to be just a necessity, and both Juliet and Marc would be primary cooks. The space would need to be tailored to the cooking style of each of them. The existing eating space was too small to be functional, appliances were outdated and in disrepair, and the storage was difficult at best.

Built in an era when space was commonly divided into large numbers of smaller rooms, this kitchen was no exception. Adjacent to the kitchen was a poorly designed and constructed storage room that had been added by the previous owners. It was ill-equipped and was not winterized, but it had possibilities and architectural interest, particularly in the original eaves and roof line that it contained. Also adjacent to the kitchen were a laundry and pantry that were inaccessible to Juliet.

The new kitchen would need to express its owners' personalities and support their modern-day lifestyle while maintaining a sense of the turn of the century. The major goals for the new design were to create a kitchen that both

Juliet and Marc could enjoy, to increase and organize the storage, and to maintain or strengthen the integrity of the home's architectural character. A comfortable place to eat or gather informally and total access for Juliet were specific objectives.

The Process

Working with both a universal kitchen designer and an architect, Juliet and Marc set out to achieve their goals. After establishing the program, conceptual plans were developed by the kitchen designer. To better utilize the overall space, activity centers were relocated. What had been the laundry and pantry became part of the main kitchen. The storeroom was winterized to incorporate laundry, storage, and a sunny eating area specific to their needs and interests.

With input and drawings from the team—the kitchen designer, the cabinet maker, the architect, and Juliet and Marc—a plan evolved. Plans were reviewed and revised by the entire team until both the aesthetics and the function of the space were complete to everyone's satisfaction. Materials were selected and reviewed for performance and appearance. By working together, the team did more than any single member could do.

The Solution

The existing high beadboard ceiling, tall windows set in brick walls, and oversized doors with transoms above established the tone for this space. Cabinetry was planned to trim out in line with the moldings between the doors and their transoms. A sense of the artisan emerged in the warmth of the natural materials used to craft the cherry cabinets, soapstone counters, stone floors, and finishing details. The simple repetition of pattern that is characteristic of the Arts and Crafts era is everywhere—in the lighting, the copper hood, the division of lights in the glass door cabinets, the wood inlay doors, and the pattern in the border of the stone floor. Although this project might have been accomplished at a more moderate cost, the richness of the materials truly resulted in a pleasure to the senses. Also noteworthy, custom solutions strengthened rather than detracted from the character of the space. The aesthetic goals were surpassed, as this is truly a gracious space.

As to function, the space was planned in detail to use judiciously the storage in Juliet's reach range. A careful review of the plan helped to determine where every needed item might best be stored, and the cabinets and backsplash were accessorized accordingly. Pull-out or fold-up work surfaces were added wherever possible. These surfaces could be used as transfer surfaces when Juliet or Marc might be accessing adjacent space. Using state-of-the-art products, timeless materials, and the skills of a fine furniture builder, the ideas could be effectively executed to strengthen rather than compromise the character of the home. In the center of the room, sufficient space was allowed for an additional work table on those occasions when it might be desired. Appliances were located for best use by both Juliet and Marc.

Although all parts of the kitchen were planned for use by both cooks, the change in counter heights and creation of knee spaces made certain areas more totally usable by Juliet. On the right side of the refrigerator, a fold-up table provides an auxiliary serving area for living and dining room meals. To the left of the refrigerator, drawer storage includes a pull-out cutting board to expand working counter space. Adjacent to the drawers the knee space is open, giving Juliet comfortable access to the refrigerator, the cooktop, a small sink, and the microwave. Although lower than customary, this microwave location allows Juliet a greater working counter. A backsplash rail system is an option for more storage at the point of use. Accessorized wall cabinets finish the storage in this area.

Across the room, 36-in-high work surfaces provide a comfortable work area for Marc when standing to cook. A recess in the cabinetry below improves Juliet's access to the sink, and a pull-out cutting board provides a work surface at a more comfortable height. Accessorized base and wall cabinets help bring more storage into Juliet's reach range. An oven with a side-swing door was installed above a pull-out work and transfer surface, with a right hinge for better access. The glass-door pantry includes another unique slide-out work surface with a beautifully crafted support, again to be used when entertaining.

What was once an unheated shed now includes a sunny eating area and organized storage specific to the needs of this household. On the inside wall a fold-up counter provides flexibility for easy maneuvering and transfer of items from the pantry. Continuing along the wall, adjustable shelves create backup pantry storage for the kitchen, and the outside wall is a closet for out-of-season clothes and equipment. The back of this space is a laundry and will eventually be a workshop, complete with front-loading laundry equipment. In the front section of what was once the shed, two large windows mimic the traditional windows of the rest of the home, with a built-in banquette and table for informal meals and chats.

Aha!

The results of careful selection of materials and design details that are rich and subtle have surpassed all expectation in creating a serene space. A surprise is the spaciousness of the new space. As Juliet says, "We had no idea that removing one wall would change the sense of space so dramatically." The banquette is truly a sunny respite. The huge main sink fits absolutely anything. The sink adjacent to the cooktop with a pull-out spray faucet is a convenience everyone appreciates. After much deliberation, soapstone was chosen for the counters, and it is more than living up to the goals set for its performance.

Always a work in progress, there are several things that Juliet and Marc might do differently. Having decided to maintain standard toekick height for the sake of storage, Juliet now finds that a raised toekick would have allowed her less concern when approaching the beautiful cabinetry. Transfer to the banquette is still being perfected.

While Juliet and Marc recognize that universal design is in some ways more an ideal than an achievable goal for each aspect of their kitchen, they are delighted with the balance in their new kitchen. There are spaces that work better for Juliet, and others that work better for Marc, resulting in an overall space that graciously suits their lifestyle.

Figure 4-3 Juliet and Marc: Kitchen work center, showing refrigerator, cooktop, and prep sink.

Figure 4-4 Juliet and Marc: Kitchen work center, showing main sink and dishwasher.

Figure 4-5 Juliet and Marc: Banquette.

Figure 4-6 Juliet and Marc: Kitchen work center, showing dishwasher, sink, oven, and pull-out work surfaces.

Figure 4-7 Juliet and Marc: Kitchen furniture, showing storage, and pull-out work surfaces.

Chapter 5

I Lost My Heart in San Francisco

HOMEOWNER: **Melanie**

CONTRACTOR: **Charles Moore**

PHOTOGRAPHER: **Jane Litz**

Background

At age 19, I traveled with my family to San Francisco, and as the song goes, I lost my heart. I planned to complete nurses' training and move to my favorite city.

In my senior year of college, a car wreck drastically altered my life. My philosophy became "Be here now," as I proceeded with life as a T7 paraplegic.

One lesson learned was that some able-bodied people are myopic in their expectations. During a job interview, a nursing supervisor declared that she could not offer me a position because I couldn't reach the medications on the upper shelves. My response was that I'd ask someone to reach it for me. Short people face such challenges every day, but the wheelchair somehow blocked the supervisor's ability to believe I could solve my own simple problems. That was the first of many such moments. As a paraplegic, my imagination must work time-and-a-half in an environment filled with barriers and obstacles. This ability enabled me to create the comfort zone that is now my home. A growing interest in furnishings and interior design also fueled my fire to make a space that would be truly mine.

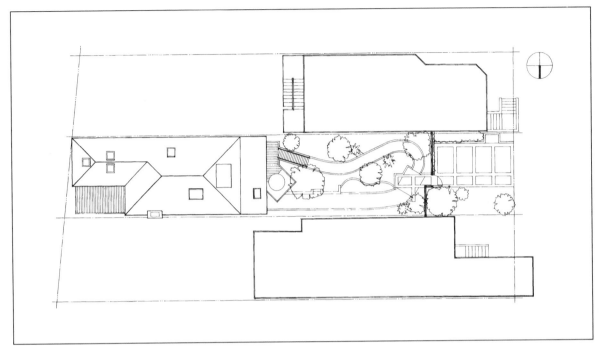

Figure 5-1 Melanie: Site plan shows ramp up 8 ft to main level.

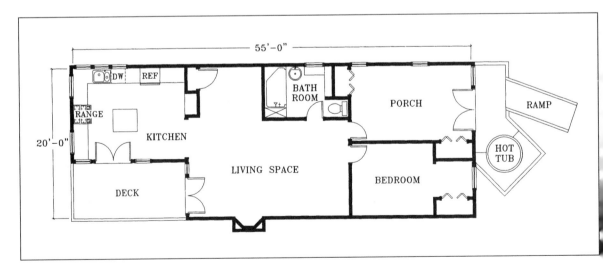

Figure 5-2 Melanie: Plan shows kitchen open to living space and activity areas, and absence of hallways.

The Challenge

My new home would need to accommodate my growing collections of antiques. It would also need to provide for my housemate, Madeline, and our huge dog. Dinner parties are frequent events for us, and I adore cooking and being with guests. The development of my kitchen was driven not only by my physical limitations but by my determination to do what I love to do. Since Madeline shares the kitchen, we had to find ways to meet the needs of two physically different individuals.

Process and Solutions

Once I found the right property, a lengthy process of adaptation began. It took 3 months to design the changes necessary and another 6 to actually do the renovations.

My team consisted of an architect with no special training in accessible design (to avoid institutional influences), an interior designer, and me. The architect was my facilitator, letting me know if the changes I wanted were do-able. Knowing what I didn't want was as important as knowing what I did want. I needed new solutions to old problems if my home was to provide me the lifestyle I sought— gracious, independent, and accommodating to friends (and dogs!).

Entry into my home was the first major problem to solve. Designing the ramp involved creating several curves to provide the extra length necessary to rise 8 ft. The solution is a little steep, so I regard the ramp as my own personal daily workout! The ramp landing is a raised deck-porch, with a hot tub and hydraulic lift near the entry.

I retained the original wood used on walls and floors throughout most of the house. Wood harmonized with the natural and organic themes I was developing, and wood floors are easy to travel.

The kitchen, naturally, became a major focus. Three skylights and large windows capture natural light and breathtaking views. Knowing what I could and could not do guided the development of the space. For example, my stove is near my sink. This allows me to slide a pot between the two. Because Madeline uses the kitchen from a standing position, most of the counters are at the usual 36-in height. Retractable doors were installed under each in anticipation of opening them for me to pull into the cavity to work.

A combination of stock items and some custom work accommodated my needs and was respectful of the budget. Stock items included pull-out shelves, pop-up shelves, and the corner Lazy Susan cabinet. Custom work, aside from lowering the cooktop and the sink, focused on storage and retrieval. Deep drawers in the lower section of the pantry cabinet held dishes and glassware traditionally stored in wall cabinets. Pull-out cutting boards were placed at various easy-access locations throughout the kitchen. The stone-look floor in the kitchen appears textured but is smooth and never impedes my movement. Was it worth the trouble and expense? You bet! Every time I entertain guests, my decisions reward me.

In the bathroom, I used a custom-designed bath chair instead of the typical side-mount deck. The chair straddles both sides of the tub, making it possible for me to simply pull up very close and lift myself onto it. When bathing, I use the extra-large deck behind the head of the tub as my landing area. With the tub filled, I have a receptive buoyant liquid to assist me in shifting my weight. When I want to soak in the tub, I just remove the seat and take a bath.

Finish materials were chosen as much for aesthetic enjoyment as for function and safety. The glass sink was the inspiration for the bathroom. For safety, heat-resistant material that does not detract from the visual experience was coiled around the trap. I found glass tile to complement the sink, and the wavelike grab bars not only work, but again evoke the ocean.

In planning renovations, I examined my daily living activities to make sure my environment would accommodate them. In the bedroom, I had to lower the rods in the closets, and I installed a buzzer, allowing me to identify and admit visitors at the front gate. Generally, I had handles lowered on the cabinetry and case pieces. Locks on the windows were lowered, too, so that I can operate them.

Furnishings also required special consideration. The bed needed to be a bit higher for ease of transfer. I dine in my armless wheelchair because it is too cumbersome to transfer when I'm hosting, shuttling in and out of the kitchen.

Aha!

In retrospect, there are a few things I might have done differently. It was surprising to find, once working in my kitchen, that I could work comfortably from a side approach. So, like most cooks, I use the cabinet bases for storage—of which there never seems to be enough!

Recognizing that as I age, my beautiful ramped entry will become decidedly more unfriendly, I recently installed a lift as a second phase, after living without one for years, allowing me the option of entering my home from the ground level.

Natural beauty and comfort are important to me; they enhance my sense of well-being. The physical challenges I have faced have been many and difficult. I have created a nest that is pleasing to look at and easy to maneuver in. It is my base; it centers and rejuvenates me for my daily life. This home is perfect for me and then some. It is consummately Melanie.

Figure 5-3 Melanie: Kitchen includes potracks, no wall cabinets, and varied-height surfaces.

Figure 5-3   Melanie: Kitchen includes potracks, no wall cabinets, and varied-height surfaces.

Figure 3-4 Irma and Jim: Curbless shower includes 13-by-13-in nonskid tiles sloped toward trough-style drain, safety-glass door, antiscald valve, varied height storage, and grab bars, and uses all universal fixtures.

Figure 4-3 Juliet and Marc: Kitchen work center, showing refrigerator, cooktop, and prep sink.

Figure 4-4 Juliet and Marc: Kitchen work center, showing main sink and dishwasher.

Figure 5-4 Melanie: Bath includes wall-hung sink, controls within reach, custom seat, and wave grab bar.

Figure 6-3   Michael and Carol: Exterior entry with inclined walk.

Figure 6-4   Michael and Carol: Integrated communal areas.

Figure 6-5   Michael and Carol: Seamless floor transitions delineate formal areas.

Figure 7-3   Pam and Harvey: Sleep area features bedroom circulation, two positioning beds, commercial carpet, broad routes, and built-in furniture.

Figure 8-3   Susan: Garden patio entry.

Figure 8-5   Susan: The bath.

Figure 9-3 David: Front entry.

Figure 9-4 David: Reception gallery features a stairlift; battery on balcony.

Figure 10-4 Doroth[y] and Rachel: The bath showing the vanity wall.

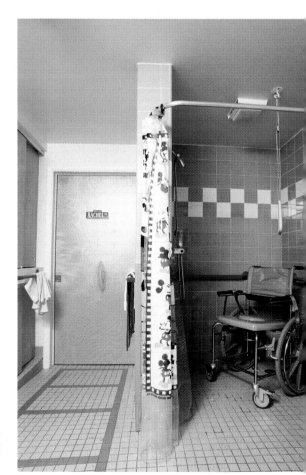

Figure 10-5 Dorothy and Rachel: The bath, showing the shower, storage, and ramped floor to secondary egress.

Figure 5-4 Melanie: Bath includes wall-hung sink, controls within reach, custom seat, and wave grab bar.

Chapter 6

A Home—A Living Sculpture

HOMEOWNERS: Carol and Michael

ARCHITECT: Chris Lassard, AIA

PHOTOGRAPHER: William Lebovich

Background

Michael and I are empty nesters now. Our home is a joy for both of us, and it supports the lifestyle we hold so dear. Open spaces and sheer volume created by soaring ceilings allow us to enjoy the Southwest art that is so much a part of our lives.

We had been living in a townhouse that became decidedly unsuitable after Michael's accident. We made reasonable adjustments to that environment, but it was still not great. As a builder and developer, Michael knew that a multilevel house with an elevator would be more cost-effective, but we wanted one-level living.

Eventually, we found a one-level home, designed 30 years earlier for a man in a wheelchair. We remodeled it, but it still wasn't our dream house. That dream house began to form on a road trip to California, when an accidental stop in Santa Fe began our passion for Southwest art. Our needs had expanded to include support not only for ourselves, but for our evolving art collection.

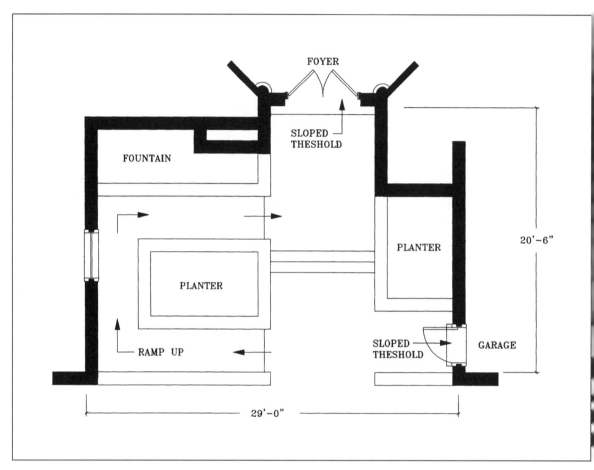

Figure 6-1 Michael and Carol: Entry.

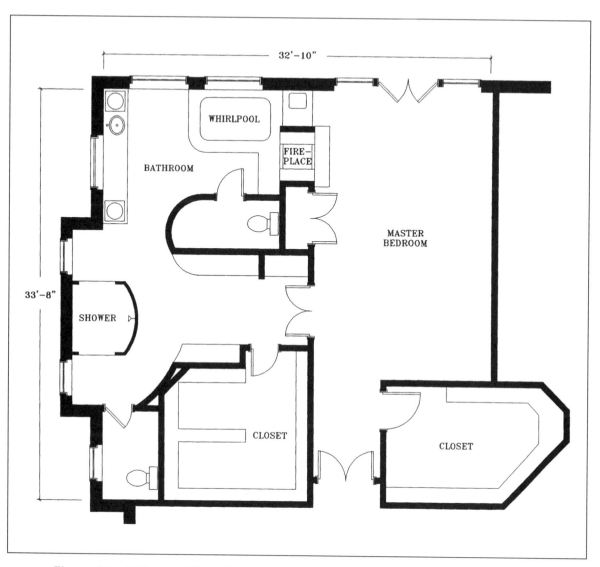

Figure 6-2 Michael and Carol: Master suite; note that toileting area design was changed in construction.

The Challenge

We had found a perfect spot on which to build our dream home. We were at an impasse in the planning when we took another trip to Santa Fe and visited a home that focused the endless possibilities. It was a 2400-sq ft home, yet it felt huge. Splendid columns bearing roof loads added excitement and drama to the space. We fell in love with the openness.

Our list of requirements grew as we imagined ourselves living and entertaining in our home. Very involved in charitable work, we often offer our home to different organizations for their fundraisers, so ample space was critical. However, for a seated user, space for its own sake is not always desirable. Although Michael uses a power chair, visitors in manual chairs would appreciate shorter travel distances. The outside of a home is the first impression others have, and ours needed to be both dramatic and accessible.

Process and Solutions

In the communal areas the house is fully open. One room flows into the next. There are no walls or doors that might impede flow except into the powder room and kitchen. The formal entertaining areas are one large unobstructed space.

Our entrance is an affirmation of how wonderful our home is for us each time we approach it from the street. It is both visually commanding and visitable. Three sumptuous curvilinear stairs lead to a large landing and towering doors. Great care was taken to integrate an inclined walkway into this courtyard approach.

Flooring materials received special attention. A variety of stone and wood surfaces were used throughout the open communal areas, in the living room in front of the fireplace, and in the kitchen.

Many adaptations to space and furniture arrangements were made because Michael uses a chair. Care was taken to arrange furniture to allow Michael to pull up to various locations without the need to move other furniture. Seamless transitions and smooth hard surfaces support ease of movement in a wheelchair, and the richness of the materials enhances and defines the space.

Other typical adaptations weren't necessary because Michael is 6 ft 4 in tall. Our kitchen counters and overhead cabinets are standard heights and sizes. Michael can reach, seated, the two lowest shelves in the overhead cabinets. Many standing users cannot reach that high. Kitchen aisles are oversized (5 ft), allowing both of us to work in the same area at the same time and enjoy the kitchen together. The stationary snack bar in the kitchen was determined by Michael's seated height.

However, the bar in the entrance foyer goes a bit further to accommodate not only Michael but also many of our friends who use chairs. It is controlled by a hydraulic system that can be raised or lowered to varying heights. It brings us joy to have all people comfortable in our home.

Michael has a very special room, his library. Some days he works out of this home office. Darkly paneled and appointed in traditional furnishings, this space offers a contrast to all the light-colored and contemporary decor evidenced in the rest of the house. It functions just as well as it looks. A soaring coffered ceiling provides the same drama as sunken floors do without creating dangerous and inaccessible transitions.

The pièce de résistance is our lower level, accessed by elevator or stairs. Sofa modules, tables, and all of the furniture are on casters and can be moved and reconfigured to permit this space to be used for a variety of activities. This furniture is, indeed, moved. We have a home theater that is rather extraordinary—candy counter, popcorn machine, marquee with twinkling lights—the whole nine yards. It was designed so that people who bring their own chairs with them can get the best seats in the house.

The bedroom is an example of how Michael's love of technology has made our home smart. A bedside terminal, which comes forward when Michael's night table drawer is open, can modulate lighting throughout the house, control the music, check the entrances, arm the alarm system, change the television channel, or talk to people in other rooms. It has made life far more manageable, as has technology in general for people with disabilities. The more efficient one's environment can be, the more time and energy a person will have to do the things that are really meaningful and important.

We wanted a comfortable bed from which Michael could get in and out with the least amount of effort. We wanted adequate room to negotiate around the bed itself, which is placed on an angle. We wanted convenience. Of course, it had to be beautiful, filled with the art we love. The position of the bed places the bathroom quite close for both of us.

We each have our separate areas in the bathroom so we don't get in one another's way. We share a unique shower. It has operable doors that are accessible from "His" and "Her" sides of the bathroom. There is a gentle curb that makes entering safer than the traditional raised curb. One wonderful timesaving device, which is integrated into our computer system, is the tub's AutoFill. Before Michael gets out of bed, he directs his computer to turn on the water and to fill the tub at a certain temperature. So, when he is ready to get in, it is ready for him.

Aha!

Many activities that we had done prior to the accident had become difficult, if not impossible, and joyless to continue once Michael was in a chair. This dream home became our miniature world. We can play pool, go swimming, work out, take a sauna, or go to the movies, right here. Few can do what we did. It has been wonderful for us to be able to diminish some of the frustrations of dealing in a world planned so exclusively for the able-bodied.

When Michael was injured, our lives were irreparably altered, or so we thought, but we are fighters. This house has provided us with a nurturing environment. It has permitted all of us a full normal life, filled with good family, good friends, good times, and greater insight and empathy. We have all been enhanced.

Figure 6-3   Michael and Carol: Exterior entry with inclined walk.

Figure 6-4 Michael and Carol: Integrated communal areas.

Figure 6-5   Michael and Carol: Seamless floor transitions delineate formal areas.

Figure 6-6 Michael and Carol: Master bedroom, view toward double-entry shower through oversized passageway.

Chapter 7

For Both of Us

HOMEOWNER: Pam and Harvey
DESIGNER: Irma Laufer Dobkin
PHOTOGRAPHER: William Lebovich

THIS SUBURBAN RAMBLER HAD UNDERGONE SEVERAL ADDITIONS AND RENOVATIONS TO make it accessible for Harvey. But it was the prospect of aging and the changes that would occur to both of them that was impetus for the last alteration.

Background

PAM

When Harvey and I married, he was in his forties, in a manual wheelchair, and working as a rocket scientist. He had lived for many years with an undiagnosed muscle disease. At first he had been able to walk, then to use a manual chair, and eventually he moved to a power chair. Accepting and making adjustments to drastic changes in one's lifestyle requires psychological fortitude and a positive outlook. When we realized that Harvey would remain in a wheelchair, we resolved to do all that we had expected we would in our lives. To meet this objective some changes were necessary; the first was to move from an apartment to a house.

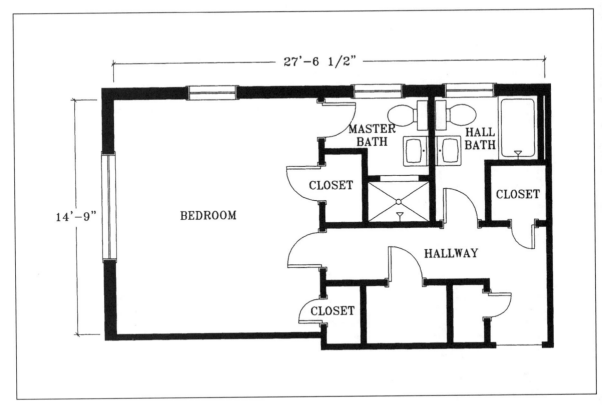

Figure 7-1 Pam and Harvey: Before floor plan.

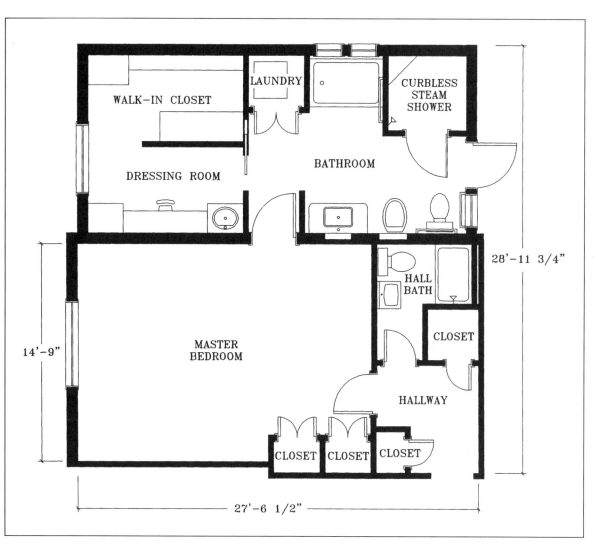

Figure 7-2 Pam and Harvey: After plan.

We found our dream house. It was on one level (no steps), had a large level lot (easier to maneuver the wheelchair), needed minor alterations for accessibility (ramps and widened doorways), and was very close to Harvey's office (no commute). We loved the tree-lined streets and multigenerational flavor of the neighborhood and knew it was where we wanted to live and raise our future children. We didn't know then, however, that this is where we would want to stay forever.

Our family grew and then grew up. When finances permitted we renovated and expanded our house, providing space and privacy for everyone. Harvey continues to enjoy his centrally located work area, where he can always be part of the family action. Cloistering or segregation in one's home was never appealing to us.

We had saved the master bedroom for last for practical and financial reasons. The original master bathroom was a compact space—and it worked well for Harvey since he could do most things for himself at first. Over time, as Harvey's mobility diminished, I became more involved in everyday assistance with bathing, dressing, and transfers. An acute situation, injuring my elbow, forced us to think about the future.

We knew that many of the things I had been able to do to assist Harvey were becoming difficult, and would continue to become more difficult with age. We began exploring options. We contacted Irma with this concern and shared with her our desire to age in place. Harvey had planned the renovation on the computer and we hired Irma to evaluate the plans. In addition, we retained an attendant to come by each weekday morning to help Harvey out of bed. He would also assist with bathing and dressing.

HARVEY

People need to realize that there are stages of disability. When my illness first evidenced itself, I was walking with a cane. Small and compact spaces were desirable. For stabilization I would steady myself as I walked by moving from one piece of furniture to another. So, close was good. When I moved into a manual wheelchair, which Pam pushed for difficult transitions such as from outside to inside or when my arms were too weak to wheel myself, close was still good but wider doorways became desirable. The chair added girth, and Pam, as small as she is, still needed some space to maneuver the chair and me into and out of the shower.

It's an interesting thing, disability. If you listen to physical therapists, they will encourage you to continue using a manual chair for as long as possible. They strongly believe that if you don't use it, you'll lose it—strength and muscle tone, that is. A broken leg provided the excuse I needed.

When I finally made the move to a power chair, I began to experience life quite differently. My power chair also freed Pam from the responsibility of pushing me around. Most of all, it freed me. Curb cuts opened the outside world to me once more. From my power chair, I can safely and fearlessly do almost everything I could prior to the onset of my illness.

The Challenge

The original master bedroom was reached by passing through the dining room and then entering an L-shaped corridor which terminated in a narrow door opening leading to the master bedroom. This passage required manipulating the wheelchair several times.

Once inside the room there was ample space in front of the bed for Harvey to maneuver to his side, which was the side closest to the bathroom. He could easily get to his armoire, where clothing was stored. However, the door to Pam's small closet blocked the route into the bathroom and barred Harvey from getting into bed or out of the room when she was using the closet. Congestion!

The bathroom entry door was 30 in wide, and its corridor was only 32 in wide. Once inside the bathroom proper, manipulation space was nearly nonexistent. The sink and toilet were in a space of less than 4 by 5 ft. Although the shower was longer than standard, it was also narrower than 3 ft. However, as most showers do, it had a 4-in curb. That meant Pam had to literally carry Harvey over the curb to get him into the shower.

Each of these conditions was a recurring annoyance for many years. The master suite renovations were intended to eliminate each of these nuisances and dangerous conditions. With all the renovations to the house over the years, the front and rear doors had gotten quite far from the bedroom. Pam and Harvey were concerned about the meandering routes in the event that there would ever be a need for a fast exit. They both wanted more pleasant and lavish surroundings to support all their activities in this area.

Process and Solutions

Most of the program requirements could be met within the parameters of the existing space. However, having lived in a cramped bedroom, they both decided that they wanted the luxury of space because it would afford the lifestyle they sought.

In the ultimate solution, a substantial 164 sq ft of interior space was added to the existing bedroom. All openings were made wider, with none less than 3 ft. The cased opening from the dining room was enlarged to a width of 42 in. The linen closet was made shallower to permit the hallway to become nearly 7 ft square. This eliminated all of the movements that were previously required to enter and turn into the two legs of the hall. Now, coming in at a diagonal required only one movement to get to the bedroom.

Harvey's side of the bed is closest to the entry door. His clothing is stored within the bedroom proper. There is a large unobstructed area to the side and front of the bed, making movement easy. Pam, too, has an ample 42-in aisle on her side closest to the window.

In the bedroom proper, appearance was especially important. They wanted it to look normal, and they wanted it dressed fashionably. Choices were driven by appearance, but each had to pass the acid test of durability, suitability, and low maintenance. Coordinated fabrics were used for window, furnishing, and bed treatments. Window treatments included convenient motorized hardware. Antiques mixed with built-ins allowed charm and function to coexist. The television was placed on a swivel base to permit it to be favorably positioned to avoid glare during daylight. The height of the set was determined based upon Harvey's position and height while in bed, as well as the span of his reach while seated in the wheelchair so that he could operate the television manually if desired.

Adjacent to the bathroom, Pam has a separate dressing room with a substantial closet. A pocket door was installed between her area and the bathroom proper. The opening is wide enough for Harvey to visit. Within the bathroom, a whirlpool with ample decking permits Pam seated and safe entry. A 5-ft square curbless shower permits Harvey to wheel into this space and then bathe without transferring. The luxurious size permits nearly indiscernible sloping toward the drain. This gentle slope provides safe purchase for the wheelchair, which would often roll on standard inclined shower floors. The full-height safety-glass shower door opens conveniently into the room and does not interfere with the toilet or bidet. All the transitions and activities that occur in this area are greatly facilitated. The shower has both overhead and hand-held showers, allowing greater flexibility in bathing and in cleanup. It also has a steam shower that is enjoyed by both.

A laundry closet was placed in the bathroom. Having the washer and dryer in this space makes laundry tasks more efficient and almost effortless, even for Harvey.

A unique solution for easier access to Harvey's sink faucets was to mount them on the front side of the counter rather than in the usual location in the back flanking the waterspout. This avoids having to reach back in order to control the water.

Aha!

PAM AND HARVEY

Our lives have been greatly improved. Everything supports ease of function. Remote controls are used for the draperies. We had adjustable beds all along, but the beautiful bed treatment made them far more appealing. Great thought was put into the practicalities of the decorative finishes. For instance, we might have wanted light beige carpeting, but it would not endure the grease that is a natural by-product of an electric wheelchair. So we installed a contract carpet used in health care facilities. It is comforting to know we can use the room with impunity and not worry about the damage the chair inflicts on fabrics and walls. We elected to go with naturally stained oak trim so that nicks and gouges would not be noticeable.

Another wonderful departure from the way we had decorated before was to have a dust ruffle. We had been concerned that no fabric could endure the might of wheels. To provide for the abuse the fabric would take, the dust ruffle was fabricated with an additional reversible fabric overlay that is secured by Velcro. When one side gets dirty, it can be reversed. In addition, the two separate dust ruffles go completely around each bed, allowing us to exchange one that is less worn with one that is more worn. It is thoughtful solutions like these that take the anxiety out of decorating. The space is appealing aesthetically. It has been fun for both of us to shop for accessories and the odds and ends that make this such a special and affirming room.

PAM

One of the most wonderful outcomes of this new space is the extra hour each weekday morning I have found. Formerly, I had to get up 1 hour earlier simply to be able to shower and dress before Harvey's assistant came to help him. Now I have the luxury of sleeping later. After bathing, I simply go into my private sanctuary and leisurely dress and groom. It is absolutely joyful to slide the pocket door shut and not to interfere or be interfered with in the morning. It can't get much better than this.

HARVEY

There are no more battles with space to fight in this room. We were really delightfully surprised by how much we enjoy having the laundry right here. Everything is efficient; no wasted time or energy. Our bedroom and bath are lovely to look at, easy to be in, and a joy for both of us.

Figure 7-3 Pam and Harvey: Sleep area features bedroom circulation, two positioning beds, commercial carpet, broad routes, and built-in furniture.

Figure 7-4   Pam and Harvey: Sink features side-mounted hot and cold handles with pipes enclosed at the left of the opening. Hot and cold supply lines are concealed behind a panel, with towel hook at point of use.

Chapter 8

The Love of Life

HOMEOWNER: Susan

ARCHITECT: Bruce Corson

PHOTOGRAPHER: Tom Ryder

THIS HOME IS BEAUTIFUL, UNIVERSAL, AND AFFORDABLE. PART OF A DEVELOPMENT IN the wine country of California, its owner, the history, the team, and the evolution of this space make a story worth telling.

Background

Susan, the owner of this home, was involved in a car accident that left her in an extended coma. She awoke with brain injuries that impacted all aspects of her life. For more than 7 years Susan has been working toward higher levels of independence, autonomy, and self-awareness, a process that is ongoing. Along with family and friends, Susan's recovery team has involved home care specialists working to strengthen Susan in body, esteem, and spirit.

Susan's changing needs and abilities, and the limitations of her surroundings, led her to look for a home that could support her. An affordable housing development was in the early stages, still on paper, when Susan and her team approached developer E. J. Wallis, his architect, and his builder. Because Califor-

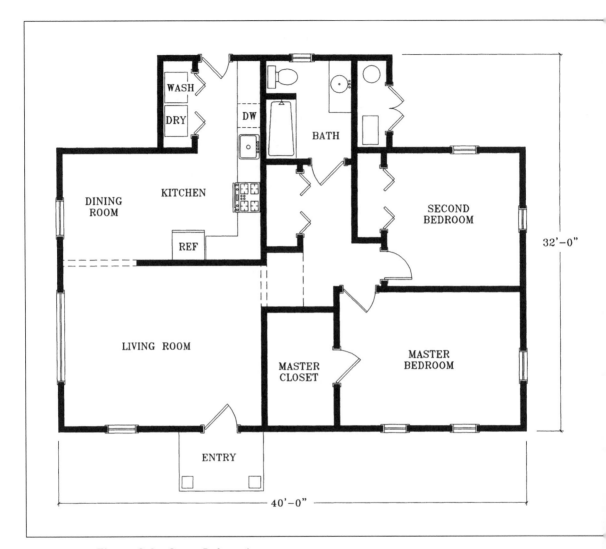

Figure 8-1 Susan: Before plan.

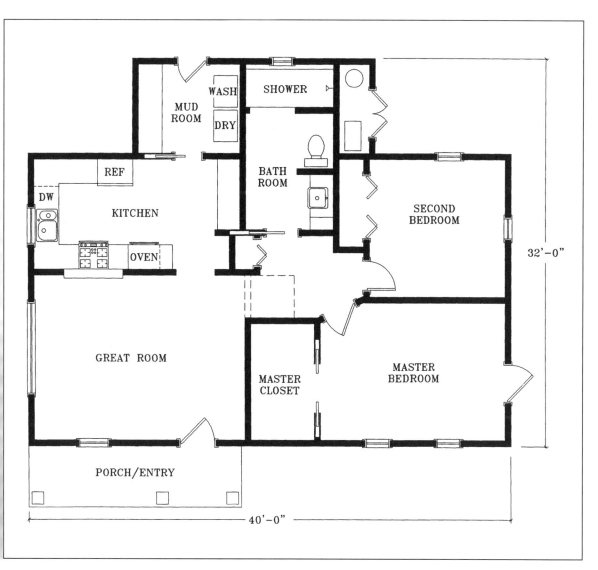

Figure 8-2 Susan: After plan.

nia law states that a buyer is not obligated to buy until the closing, any changes made for accessibility could be considered a risk to the builder and developer. To their credit, this team was not only willing but gracious in joining Susan, setting her well-being as their goal.

The Challenge

Within the parameters of the development and the house plan designed by project designer Mr. Breashears, architect Bruce Corson was retained to work with the team to meet Susan's needs. While the accident had changed many things for Susan, it did not take away her sociable nature and her love of light and open spaces. Susan had strength, but not balance, and her right side was her stronger side. For Susan, access began with being able to see and order the components of a task, so line of sight was important. Susan used a power chair to get about. Priorities included a sense of welcome, openness, and light, as well as creation of an environment supportive to Susan that would blend with the emerging community. The cost of the recommended changes was critical to Susan, and, because this was to be affordable housing, it was also critical to the developer.

The Process

Builder Geary Ray and architect Bruce Corson worked with a total commitment to meeting Susan's needs within the guidelines of the project. The land was incredibly valuable, and with no protection for the developer, as previously mentioned, the need to be on target both functionally and aesthetically was critical. This team went a long way toward demonstrating the value of universal design that must be realized in the construction industry.

A priority list with prices attached was developed as major revisions to the home entry and interior were proposed. With a short time frame, cooperation and total commitment to Susan's needs were critical, and they were there. A look at the original plan and the redesign shows the wonderful results of these efforts.

The Solution

On approaching this home one gets a sense of welcome, enhanced by the enlarged front porch, which doubles as a landing for level entry into the home. Both the front and back entries were changed to allow access for Susan. A back patio was created, including access to the carport and to a path around the side of the house. In time an accessible garden was developed, so Susan could continue to indulge her love of growing things. A fire exit door replaced a window in Susan's bedroom. Traffic patterns within the house were streamlined to eliminate unnecessary wheelchair maneuvering and contribute to the feeling of openness.

Having worked in the gourmet food business, Susan's ability to access and operate in the kitchen was a priority. The dining room was eliminated to allow for a more generous kitchen space. A window or pass-through was created between the kitchen and the new great room, eliminating the need for Susan to transport food on her lap. The benefits of this change also included allowing her to see between the two rooms. It afforded her care provider both visual and acoustical contact with Susan when they would be on opposite sides of the partition. Within the kitchen, generous knee spaces and pantry roll-out shelves provided easy access. Changing from a range to a cooktop and oven allowed for installation at appropriate heights. A grab bar or rail installed under the front edge of the countertop provided support. The entire layout was geared for Susan's stronger right side. A desk in the kitchen and the redesign of the mud room provided space for Susan and her support team to create a generous area for the ordering of tasks so important to her growing independence.

In the bathroom, the space was expanded and realigned with a left corridor, allowing Susan to rely on her stronger right side. The expanded vanity area included full knee space and, again, room for ordering tasks. The toileting area included reinforced walls for existing and future support systems. While still open, the wall arrangement also provided privacy in this area. Even if the bathroom door was left open, a person using the facilities would be protected from view. A roll-in shower was created with room for Susan and a care provider as needed. This became a space that has truly enhanced Susan's independence in all bathroom activities.

The master bedroom required minimal but valuable changes. The side window was changed to a door for quick egress in case of emergency. Double pocket doors were installed at the closet so that Susan could easily enter and see the entire space.

In the great room, a recliner chair is now Susan's command central. From here, she can experience the wonderful light while she eats or writes or relaxes. She can see through to most of the rest of the house, and can be an active participant in living.

Throughout the house, well-planned natural and electric light is abundant. The impact of this generous light, along with the openness of the new plan, is a sense of cheerful and open space.

Aha!

In Susan's words, her home is "perfectly supportive." An unexpected benefit of the change is the wonderful sense of expansiveness. By design, the new space is consummately functional, but it is Susan who brings vitality to this home. A lover of life, Susan's bright countenance is felt everywhere. Collections of stars, apples, and zebras testify to her positive spirit. As her home care team leader Dale said, "Home is where we connect with comfort and joy," and in this home the source of that joy is Susan. Both this home and its owner have a sense of living that, once experienced, can never be forgotten.

Aha! and More

In the year since Susan was first visited by the authors, her characteristic "big energy" has been focused on expanding her approach to life. As the team says, "by pushing beyond the comfort zone," Susan now walks with some support and is more free to enjoy her home independently.

Just outside her home, Susan's back patio includes a container garden where she nurtures vegetables to harvest. The entire patio area is now a source of pleasure and comfort. Beyond her patio, Susan's love of people is shared with others in her neighborhood, where households support and enjoy each other, living out the true meaning of community.

Susan shares the warmth of her home today with a housemate. Joe, age 42, continues to recover from a stroke that occurred 7 years ago, and he also benefits from the gracious support of the design. Spacious rooms and passageways, wide doors, and smooth transitions enhance participation in household activities for the housemates. Both Susan and Joe enjoy the positive energy in this space and the effort each is making to move toward full independence.

Figure 8-3 Susan: Garden patio entry.

Figure 8-4   Susan: View from front entry.

Figure 8-5 Susan: The bath.

Chapter 9

Dreams Realized

HOMEOWNERS: **David, Elsie, and Cornish**
DESIGN/BUILD/CONTRACTOR: **Chuck Fischer**
PHOTOGRAPHER: **Mark Lohman**

DAVID WAS JUST COMPLETING HIS EDUCATION AND MEDICAL RESIDENCY WHEN AN accident rearranged his life and his plans for it. After living as a quadriplegic in a home full of barriers, David and his parents began the search for a home that might support and accommodate them with only minor adjustments. The search was fruitful, resulting in the purchase of a beautiful Spanish-style Southern California home. It is a home that embraces universal design subtly and graciously.

The Challenge

The needs of this household included space to support three working adults and a full-time attendant. With a practice outside the home, David still required a work space at home. Cornish, a minister, also needed a home office with substantial work area. His mother, Elsie, wanted space for her computer and "millions of books." A bedroom for the attendant close to David's bedroom was essential. To make this house a home, David's love of music required considera-

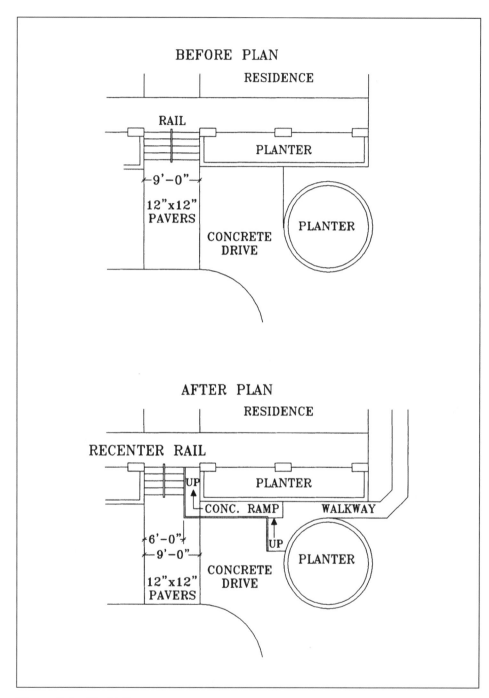

Figure 9-1 David: Front entry.

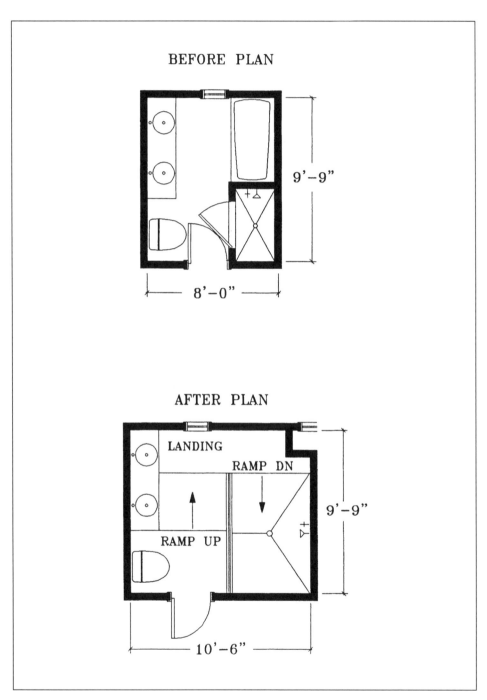

Figure 9-2   David: Bathroom.

tion. Sociable and outgoing, David and his parents enjoyed entertaining and hoped to continue their tradition of casual outdoor gatherings. It was important that David have access to all spaces in the house—that it be totally his home.

Process and Solutions

The home the family found met their needs, with what they considered to be only minor alterations, and so they explored their options and the revisions were planned. First they hired Chuck Fischer, a design-builder with a willingness to push the envelope. Next, they hunted for products and solutions. A two-story, their new home had previously been owned by a family with five children, and the space was generous. Hallways were unusually wide, and access to all parts of the house was open to all family members if the staircase could be dealt with.

The changes began with widening doorways. The thresholds at the French doors to the upper porch and at the lower patio were inclined. A gently sloping ramp at one entry was added to deal with the change in levels between the living and dining room.

In David's bath, the tub and shower was replaced with a roll-in shower. By moving the common wall, borrowing 2 ft from the adjacent attendant's room, the shower was also enlarged. The floor was sloped up to the shower entrance and back down to the drain. A fixed glass panel was added to separate the shower area from the rest of the bathroom. No changes were needed at the toilet or lavatory, but changing to a gooseneck faucet cut down on water on the floor.

The kitchen required minimal changes to suit the needs of the household. The hall floor tile was trimmed and the wood floor was sanded to create a more gradual change at the threshold. Although David enjoys grilling, he did not wish to be the main cook for the family. By placing the island on casters, the space plan of the kitchen was opened enough to provide full access. A preexisting 30-in-high snack bar worked beautifully for the entire household, including David's supervision of meal preparation.

The front entrance, a beautiful statement of the gracious style of the home, was altered to incorporate a ramp. In the process a step-free path was created around the house to the pool and cabana. It was important to maintain the aesthetics of the gardens and front entry. This goal was accomplished by tiling the surface of the ramp to look like an extension of the porch.

The crowning glory of this home is its two-story entry and reception gallery, with a gracious sweeping curved staircase leading to a balcony and living space on the second floor. A stairlift was selected that integrated beautifully with the ironwork of the railing. A battery was installed to automatically kick in, in case of power loss. A paddle control on the left of the lift would allow improved access in case of an emergency. In addition, an independent track chair was purchased, operated by rechargeable batteries.

On the second level, David's music and work space remained open to the balcony and reception gallery below. A high-tech computer station was created to support his work and social activities. A mouthstick rather than a mouse could be used to control the computer, which in turn could control music, including a 200-disc CD changer. In the bedroom, David's voice could control the lights, fan, and radio.

This family's lifestyle fit naturally into the home. Downstairs a game room became a library for Elsie's books and work area. A sleep sofa allowed this space to double as guest room. What was once a maid's room became a guest room with private bath. The utility room provided large amounts of storage space for David's equipment needs and supplies. There was sufficient storage space to order these supplies in 3-month quantities. A barber-style sink and good light helped to create good space for Elsie to act as family barber. To provide for nighttime snacks, a refrigerator and appropriate dish storage were added.

Aha!

David practices medicine. In spite of the dramatic changes that were forced on him, David and his family realized their dreams with the help of this supportive and gracious home.

Figure 9-3 David: Front entry.

Figure 9-4   David: Reception gallery features a stairlift; battery on balcony.

Figure 9-5 David: Rear path to pool.

Chapter 10

Mother and Daughter

HOMEOWNERS: Dorothy and Rachel

DESIGNER: Mary Jo Peterson

CONTRACTOR: R. Dale Ziegler

PHOTOGRAPHER: Willam Lebovich

THE GOAL OF THIS REMODELING PROJECT WAS TO IMPROVE RACHEL'S QUALITY OF LIFE and the wonderful result is that it has done so not only for her, but for the entire family. With the caring and the skills of Rachel, her family, and the professionals involved, the evolution of this space can be an inspiration to all.

Background

This home is lived in by a typical American family, with a few twists. Rachel, age 15, lives with her mom, Dorothy, a widow, and her 16-year-old brother, Ari, with occasional visits from her adult brother and sister. Dorothy works and teaches outside the home and has the usual accompanying shortages of time and energy. Ari and Rachel are in school during the day, and all three contribute to the household in their off time.

One of the twists to this family involves the incredible personalities of both mother and daughter. Dorothy's philosophy is to enjoy everything life has to offer, to "have fun at what you're doing and you'll be doing a good job." Rachel's

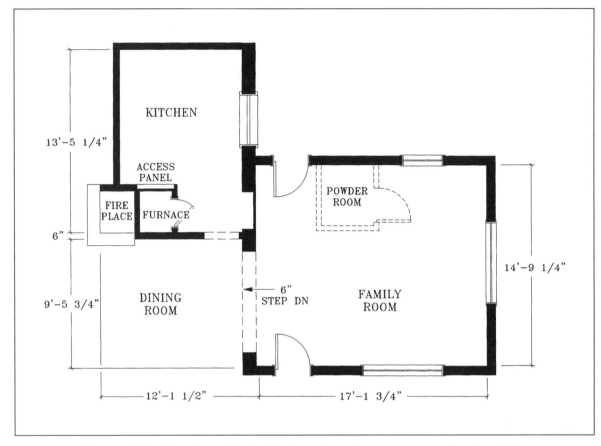

Figure 10-1 Dorothy and Rachel: Before plan, with narrow entries, floor-level changes, and maneuvering nightmares.

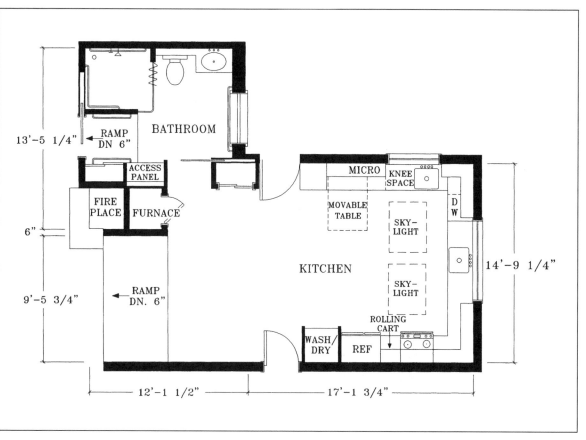

Figure 10-2 Dorothy and Rachel: Solution plan is an open plan, featuring maximum-width entries, storage at point of use, ramped floor areas, and bath support systems.

philosophy, in keeping with family tradition, is to "smile a lot, laugh, and be happy." Both enjoy the garden, and Rachel also loves the typical teenage activities.

Another twist to this family is that at age 2, Rachel was diagnosed with spastic quadriplegic cerebral palsy. The impact of this on the household and the desire to support Rachel in the activities she enjoys prompted changes in their living space.

The Challenge

While there are many things that Rachel enjoys doing herself, there are also times when she needs assistance. She uses a power wheelchair with a joystick control at her right hand. Having limited balance, she is able to stand with maximum aid to transfer, and to speak up to direct her care. She requires help in personal grooming and dressing. A care provider helps Rachel prepare for bed and assists her at other times.

At the time of the renovation, Rachel's size was putting added physical stress on Dorothy. The lack of maneuvering space and support prevented both Dorothy and Rachel from doing what they could to manage Rachel's activities in the bathroom. Both the kitchen and the bath were full of barriers. The main household bathroom had a 24-in door. The kitchen was small, with a narrow S-bend at the entry, making it a wheelchair-negotiating nightmare. When Rachel was at the kitchen table, even in her pediatric chair, it became all but impossible to access the refrigerator or to move in the kitchen. With three interior walls, one window, and the heating system adjacent, the kitchen was too hot and too closed in for access or comfort. The existing combination family room and office included an inaccessible powder room and much storage for things no longer being used regularly. It was up one step from the rest of the house, creating another barrier to free movement.

The family wanted Rachel to have a space in which to be more independent. Reflection on the difficulties of daily living spawned the idea of converting the small, warm kitchen into a spacious bath, and the seldom-entered family room into a spacious and light kitchen. Priorities were durability, access, and ease of maintenance. A January freeze, thaw, and rain caused structural damage to the cinderblock-on-slab construction of the house, and prompted action to improve both the aesthetics and function of the space.

Process and Solutions

A team was gathered to accomplish these goals. Included in the team were family members, bringing great personal experience and skills (including Rachel's sister, Betsy, a pediatric physical therapist); a kitchen and bath designer with expertise in universal and accessible design; and a remodeling contractor with skill, patience, and a willingness to try new ideas. All had a total commitment to Rachel. Taking a year from start to finish, the team worked to create a beautiful and supportive environment within the parameters of a lean budget, a need to totally change the space, and an assessment of Rachel's present and future abilities. Through cooperation and due diligence this was achieved.

The kitchen is now the hub of the house. On entering the front door, four large windows at the end of the room and the two skylights draw people to the light of the kitchen. There are doors, one to either side of the kitchen, that lead outside to the garden, also seen through the windows. The room is so open and airy that no outside patio is really needed—this kitchen has succeeded in bringing the outside in. The family hoped to create the feeling of a conservatory filled with plants and sunlight. The expansive views of the garden and an ample use of house plants help to achieve this goal.

Natural light in abundance was a priority when planning the kitchen. As it exists now, the room is sunny throughout the day and is brightly lit by the setting afternoon sun. The new bathroom, adjacent to the furnace, is the warmest room in the house. It, too, has a window that receives the afternoon sun. By starting from the slab up, the family room turned kitchen is no longer threatened by unpredictable weather. The enhanced landscaping in the backyard improves both function (drainage) and aesthetics.

In planning, the team, including the occupational therapist, tried to project Rachel's potential and plan for things they wanted her to do, things they hoped she would be able to do in the future, and things that they definitely did not want her to do, such as use the oven. Expectations were initially met in both the bathroom and the kitchen, yet they continue to change as Rachel discovers more tasks she can accomplish independently.

The Bath

The main entry to the bath is oversized, using the maximum space available. The vanity area is set at a height that clears Rachel's chair, with a shallow sink, a mirror and a "banjo" top to provide easy access to both Rachel and the other ladies of the house. A standard-height commode with an elevated seat with integral grab bars allows adjustments in height for Rachel's changing needs. The roll-in shower has wall-mounted grab bars and ceiling-mounted trapeze grips, improving Rachel's ability to maneuver in and out of the shower chair and the shower. A second location for the trapeze gives Rachel added support for transfer at the commode. Storage, both concealed for private hygiene products and open for other bath supplies, is maximized.

Rolling storage for Rachel's use when at the vanity again increases her independence. A second entry exists at the end of a down ramp, for ease of egress directly to her bedroom after evening bathing, and for use in case of emergency.

The Kitchen

The washer and dryer are easily approached and accessed by all. The side-by-side refrigerator places some storage in both refrigerator and freezer within everyone's reach. The rolling cabinet cart adjacent to the refrigerator makes transfer of items easier for all. Rachel's access to the range is negligible, as this is an area she is best not using. The work areas moving through the main sink and dishwasher are planned mainly for use by Dorothy and others. The elevated dishwasher is easier on Dorothy's back and is a better height for Rachel's access. Cubbies and storage on the third wall of the kitchen are accessible to Rachel. A shallower sink allows her chair to clear, and the windows are set at heights that improve the views for Rachel and others. Storage for her most-used items is provided on either side of the movable table, which serves as a work surface for Rachel and a dining table for all. Elimination of the apron on one side of the table allows

Rachel to pull under it without adjusting her joystick. The toaster oven and microwave are conveniently located on a counter just above the table for all to use. The table can be rolled out and relocated for occasional larger affairs.

These changes and additions have allowed Rachel more independence in her daily activities. She can now move into and around the bathroom and the shower more independently, and she can drive her chair under the new vanity, to assist with washing and tooth care. In the kitchen, Rachel can now pull under the table without assistance, heat up items in the microwave and toaster oven, wash dishes in her lowered sink, load and unload the raised dishwasher, get ice and water from the outside of the freezer door, use some of the cabinets and drawers in the kitchen, and help with laundry. The carpetless floors allow her greater ease in propelling her manual wheelchair. The stop or change in level between the main part of the house and the kitchen and bath area, which had been hazardous, could not be eliminated. The risks involved were minimized by sloping the entire floor between these rooms. Rachel's driving has become less stressful (i.e., less yelling from her mom) with the addition of wider doorways, pocket doors, and carpeted wall areas.

Aha!

The changes made have impacted on the entire family—the boys now have their own bathroom that can remain a bachelor's pigsty without upsetting the others. The girls' bathroom stays cleaner, is easier to shower Rachel in, and allows more space for Rachel's wheelchair, attendant, shower chair, and storage. The improved utilization of space was realized when all of Rachel's class came over for a pizza party. The kitchen was able to accommodate eight wheelchairs and at least eight other people (including the plumber who was putting the finishing touches on the kitchen sink, and grandmom and grandpop) without crowding, congestion, gridlock, or wheelchairs crashing into walls. On another occasion, 30 people were accommodated at an open house. It has become a model of universal design—Rachel's orthopedic surgeon sends his patients' parents to see this wonderfully responsive home when they are contemplating home modifications.

Figure 10-3 Dorothy and Rachel: The kitchen is spacious and light for function and aesthetics.

Figure 10-4   Dorothy and Rachel: The bath, showing the vanity wall.

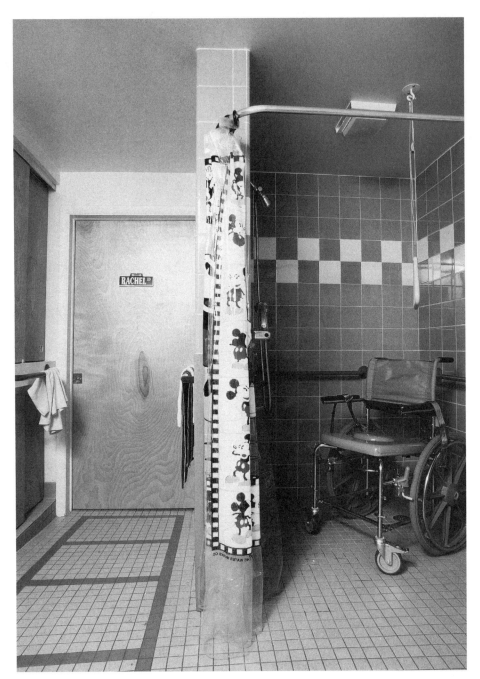

Figure 10-5   Dorothy and Rachel: The bath, showing the shower, storage, and ramped floor to secondary egress.

Chapter 11

Synchronicity

HOMEOWNER: Jim
ARCHITECT: Nick Noyes
PHOTOGRAPHER: Chris Irion

THIS HOME IS IN PERFECT HARMONY WITH ITS SURROUNDINGS AND ITS OWNER. SET IN 13 acres of coastal meadow just 4 miles from the ocean and 1200 ft above it amidst redwoods and coastal woodlands, it is home to Jim, his two dogs, and all the natural life that such a setting would support.

The Background

When a horrific accident left Jim paralyzed from the waist down, with no function in his lower body and chronic pain as a constant, life simply didn't work for a while. He was forced to reexamine his living space, his work, and his approach to life.

Having known the sea to be a place of healing, he turned his work to involvement with indigenous people and their watercraft. Today, he researches traditional methods of construction and use of watercraft among Native American and Inuit tribes. He then works with them to bring back these aspects of their past, and in the process eliminates barriers between cultures that have been sep-

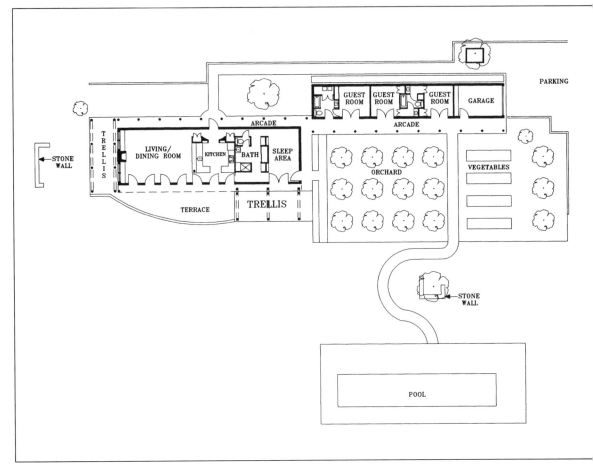

Figure 11-1 Jim: House plan.

arated by time or sea. As Jim says, "In a kayak, I can knife through the waves, dance upon the sea, and be swift and silent." Relying on his upper body strength, he is not held back by the lack of function in his lower body. Again, the power of the sea to renew the spirit brought Jim to purchase the land he now calls home. His comment was that he and this land were meant to be together—a perfect fit. On this site, Jim and his brother, architect Nick Noyes of San Francisco, worked to create a home that would support Jim's evolving lifestyle.

The Challenge

Jim enjoys being host to family and friends, but with chronic pain as a physical reality, he also needs to be able to separate himself somewhat from guests, setting several interesting demands on the space. It needed to be open and spacious for easy maneuvering, with space for guests and with provisions for privacy.

Because his work involves so much research, Jim would need a place for books, computer, and "office" kinds of things. With pain a constant in Jim's life, this space would need to include flexibility for comfort. His interest in the outdoors and things natural also deserved attention in the design process.

At over 6 ft, Jim's height and great upper body strength impacted the design in several ways. Easily accessed storage was needed for equipment and medical supplies. The range within his reach is greater than most, and the space he occupies as a seated person is also extended.

Process and Solutions

Jim and his brother Nick worked together to create what began as a weekend retreat, and evolved into Jim's full-time home. Then still an undergraduate, Nick worked from instinct and caring to design a house that would be the essence of what Jim needed.

The plan was for one level with straight lines and broad passages. The main building houses living/dining, kitchen, and bedroom suite for Jim. Oversized glazed doors let in sunshine and frame the incredible views. Beautiful concrete floors retain heat, taking advantage of the passive solar opportunities this climate provides. Outside the kitchen door, a walkway leads to the second building, which houses three guest suites and the garage. Together the structures are reminiscent of turkey barns, familiar to the area.

Nick planned the outdoor spaces to be an integral part of Jim's daily living. In his words, "It was important to create a variety of outdoor spaces so that Jim would not have to go far to experience different worlds." On the west, there is a trellised pergola, allowing a view to the sea. On the south, a second terrace, partially shaded by a trellised cap, extends living space and provides views of the hot tub and pool, and of the orchard to the east. Both the orchard and the raised flower and vegetable gardens to the east of the main house provide access, active participation, sustenance, and beauty.

In both indoor and outdoor living space, Jim moves with little effort due to subtle consideration of doors and doorways, passageways, maneuvering spaces, and the general openness of the plan. The scale of the home naturally supports the oversized doors, windows, and passageways. The combination bedroom and research center allows Jim to work from his waterbed if he chooses, with the doors and windows open to the vast view of orchard, garden, and beyond. In nonwork time, he moves easily through gardening, cooking, or other daily activities.

The guest building has answered his need for privacy, easy access, and guest space. The hot tub and pool are down a gently sloping pathway, providing a workout for his upper body and refreshment for his spirit.

Aha!

This home is remarkable for its subtle approach to universal design. It blends indoors and out as seamlessly as it combines comfort and minimum effort for Jim with an atmosphere cordial to any guest. Referring to this, Jim calls the house his "invisible partner, making life so effortless that I forget I'm using a chair." Traveling is a brutal reminder of how disabling an environment can be, and reinforces his appreciation for home.

As a place to live, this home goes beyond all expectations. The purpose for raising the vegetable and flower gardens was access. The *Aha!* was that they also provided a sculptural elegance and a way to block out garden pests, so well that Jim's parents have now created similar raised gardens at their home. The results of emphasis on passive solar in the materials and design surpassed expectations. Areas like doors and passageways that were oversized for access have brought the structure into harmony with the surroundings. The simplicity of these solutions speaks to Nick's sensitivity as an architect, and his ability to blend what nature provided with what Jim needed in terms of both physical and spiritual support. It is truly a gracious space, and by the way, it is totally accessible.

Figure 11-2 Jim: A view to the kitchen, showing openness and ease of movement.

Figure 11-3   Jim: Raised flower and vegetable gardens.

Figure 11-4 Jim: Combination bedroom and work space softens the line between indoors and out.

Chapter 12

On My Own

HOMEOWNER: Scott
DESIGNER: Irma Laufer Dobkin
PHOTOGRAPHER: William Lebovich

Background

When I was diagnosed with chronic progressive multiple sclerosis in the summer of 1984, I heard about some of the difficulties that could be in store for me. I did not, of course, want to consider any of those things. I was simply relieved to finally know the cause of the difficulty I was having in running and, occasionally, losing my balance while walking. At that time I couldn't manage to think about what might lie ahead for me. I resolved instead to overcome potential setbacks by swimming regularly. Removing me further from any consideration of multiple sclerosis was the exciting prospect of having landed a great job. A Washington-based magazine offered me a position in its New York bureau. Being familiar with New York, I confidently headed off to the big city.

Nevertheless, MS did, in fact, progress, and as new needs pressed themselves on me, I began to learn just how inaccessible the inexpensive walk-up in which I was living was becoming for me. Therefore, I moved across the street into a building with an elevator. Gradually, over the next 11 years, I had to move several times in order to find more accessible apartments as my illness advanced.

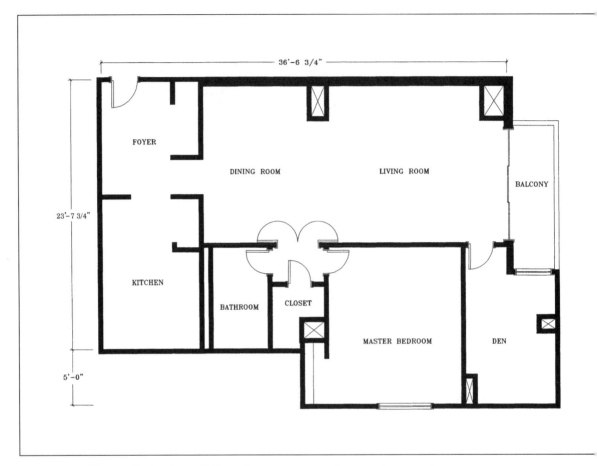

Figure 12-1   Scott: Before plan, with narrow doors and congestion at passage.

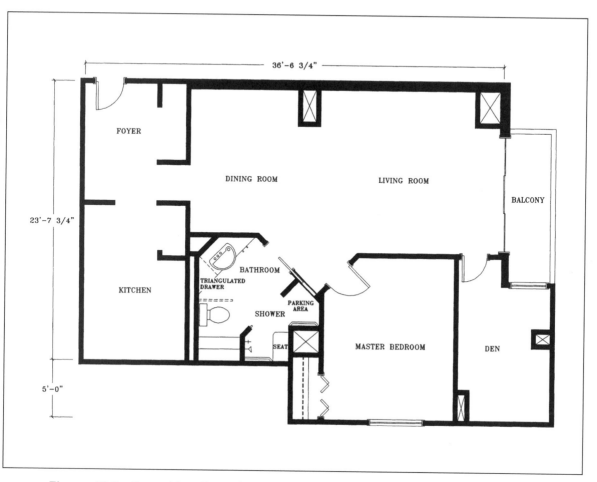

Figure 12-2 Scott: After floor plan, with pocket door entry, curbless shower, and drawer storage for personal garments.

None of the amenities found in these apartments, however, could obviate the taxation and energy drain that the trek, whether to work or to the pool to which I belonged, had on me.

The disease marched on. First one cane, then two, and by 1991, I was getting around in a scooter. This mobility aid, my scooter, was both liberating and confounding. The confounding part—entrances were now too narrow and required careful steering; shelves and tables now required careful tact and attention if they were to remain standing and in one piece. This was the beginning of my education in what an accessible living space should be.

Disability and the subsequent mobility impairments are hard to imagine. I have made a study of entrances. Most are decidedly unfriendly. Imperfect entries are tremendous barriers for people in scooters or wheelchairs. If there is a level entry, the first impediment encountered is the width of the doorways. Entry width can deter a seated user from even entering a room, or if the entrance is just wide enough to allow you in, it can still catch one of your wheels, thereby causing you to fishtail into a wall. Seated, every turn requires maneuvering. These things can be avoided, of course, with reasonable and considered planning on the part of the person in a chair or scooter, but who wants to spend such time entering or exiting a room?

The bathroom has always been the most difficult space to negotiate. In my last New York apartment I would have to carefully steer into an entranceway between a closet and the bathroom door. Once there, I would then twist and land either on the commode or on a bench in front of the sink. I managed to land correctly about 98 percent of the time. However, the 2 percent of unsuccessful transfers began to weigh on me. Despite the pride I felt at being able to hop from my scooter and accomplish the gymnastic pivot and fall either onto the toilet, bench, or floor, I was concerned.

In appraising my independent living situation with friends, focus was placed on making transitions easier and safer. We decided that I was running the serious risk of losing my balance and falling in the bathroom among inherently unforgiving surfaces. In addition, I was spending an inordinate amount of time, energy, and effort traveling eight blocks to and from the Y, changing, swimming, and changing once again in order to get the only whole-body exercise I could.

The Challenge

The best course of action, it seemed, was to find a condominium—that is, an apartment that could be adapted to my specifications and that had a swimming pool. Given the expenses involved in such a move, I decided to explore Washington, D.C., where my family resided, to look for a new apartment. My priorities were simple: I wanted to live in a building with a pool, near a subway stop. Of course, the apartment had to have a large, accessible bathroom, and it could not have tight, challenging spaces that would require time-consuming maneuvering.

Process and Solutions

It would be hard to imagine obtaining an apartment that would meet all those requirements in this day and age, but my parents and I did. Apartment living being all on one level or accessible by elevator solved one challenge. The apartment we found needed some modification, mainly simplifying and widening routes and doorways, to enable me to live independently at little risk to my safety and well-being.

What would make this apartment work for me would be having that one space that everyone has to visit several times a day—the bathroom—be totally accessible. Even though I had grown used to the gymnastics involved in entering and exiting bathrooms, I loathed it every time nature called. A negotiable bathroom requires space to maneuver and transfer either to the commode or the shower. By annexing space from an adjacent walk-in closet and combining both to create a larger single bathroom, my dream bath emerged. The new plan included a diagonal wall, providing space for a pocket door and a direct route to the toilet. The sink, to the right of the entry, was also placed diagonally, eliminating its intrusion into my turnaround space.

Other changes made the enlarged space even more usable: a fold-down support bar next to the commode and a vertical grab bar on the edge of the shower wall closest to the commode. These strategically placed grab bars provided two handholds that made transfers a snap.

Given the fixed drain location, the shower setup configuration was ideal. Initially, it appears enormous. The cased opening is nearly 4 ft wide. In actuality, the shower is compartmentalized into a parking area for my scooter and the shower itself. For convenience, towels, robes, and removed attire are hung from large hooks in the parking area. A chrome shelf stores large towels. In the shower itself, everything is within arm's reach. Opposite the built-in seat to which I transfer, a vertical bar holds a removable hand-held showerhead. Controls are within easy reach of the entry, so I can adjust it before entering if I want.

It removed the trying task of hurling myself onto a bench straddling the two sides of a bathtub. Bathing now involves simply parking my scooter close to the built-in shower seat and transferring onto it using another grab bar and an arm of my scooter. Additional provisions were made to afford me independence, safety, and convenience. Where the tub had been, base and overhead cabinets for storage were installed. The lower drawers hold toilet supplies and personal clothing. It is fairly standard for people with mobility aids to dress and undress in the bathroom. The apron (the horizontal rail under the countertop) of the open cabinet area near the toilet holds the toilet paper dispenser. The area below that was left open to house a clothesbasket.

A drawer base placed to the left side of my sink counter closest to the commode stores all my grooming supplies. Easy-to-reach storage, coupled with an ample pull-in space under the sink, finally made brushing my teeth, washing my hands, and shaving infinitely easier. I no longer risk losing my balance while craning over a sink, trying to reach implements and controls.

I spend most of my time researching investments in a den that has been converted into an office. In this room (approximately 6 by 10 ft), less space works better for me. I have enough space to execute a three-point turn, so I never feel closed in. A desk along a 5-ft stretch of wall, which has a large file drawer, a file cabinet, and a book shelf behind me, places everything I need within arm's reach.

Aha!

An unexpected benefit of the changes was that the unusual angled walls made the overall space far more interesting than just having long straight walls. The

Figure 11-2 Jim: A view to the kitchen, showing openness and ease of movement.

Figure 11-3 Jim: Raised flower and vegetable gardens.

Figure 11-4 Jim: Combination bedroom and work space softens the line between indoors and out.

Figure 12-4 Scott: Bath entry; bath features storage near toilet.

Figure 12-5 Scott: Shower and toilet.

Figure 13-3 Karen and Jack: Front exterior entrance with visitable inclined path.

Figure 13-5 Karen and Jack: Bathtub, showing the deck with storage, and camel–and–palm tree tile art.

Figure 14-4 Faulkner Project: Antefoyer features low-maintenance solar materials and provides a thermal barrier without need for level changes.

Figure 15-2 Peterson project: The GE Real Life Design Kitchen.

Figure 16-3 IFDA Kennedy House: Kitchen features combined open kitchen and dining area, large tactile phone, and generous and accessible storage and work areas.

Figure 16-4 IFDA Kennedy House: Chuck's bath features fold-down support arm, curbless shower, and vanity sink in bedroom area.

Figure 16-5 IFDA Kennedy House: Hall bath features shallow tub, fold-down tub seat, high toilet, fold-down support arm, and transom.

Figure 18-2   DeLaura project: The Jesse Owens kitchen.

Figure 19-2   Peterson project: The GE Living Center.

Figure 19-5 Peterson project: Computer center designed for flexible use.

Figure 19-7 Peterson project: Island features seating, movable table, microwave at table height, and open storage.

door into the office was also widened to permit easier and safer access. Having all the doors 3 ft wide made them look standard.

Living independently is important. As the MS progresses, I become less certain that I can remain living alone. Presently, the changes that were made in the physical environment allow me to live independently. That brings me great satisfaction. In the future, despite the alterations, I may not be able to go it alone. No one looks forward to these types of status changes, but they are less disruptive if they have been considered. There is a daybed in the den for an assistant. When the bathroom was redesigned, consideration was given to the needs of a standing shower user. For now, I operate independently and that is great!

Figure 12-3   Scott: Sink area.

Figure 12-4   Scott: Bath entry; bath features storage near toilet.

Figure 12-5   Scott: Shower and toilet.

Figure 12-6   Scott: Shower.

Chapter 13

Freedom of Space and Spirit

HOMEOWNERS: Karen and Jack
DESIGNER: Belinda McClure, IFDA
ARCHITECT: Craig Stewart, AIA
PHOTOGRAPHER: William Lebovich

ON HER 61ST BIRTHDAY, KAREN READ AN ARTICLE IN THE *WASHINGTON POST* HOME Section called "Aging-in-Place," authored by Irma Dobkin. It described how homes could create barriers for the less than perfectly able-bodied. It prompted her to evaluate not only her home but also the direction of her life.

Background

Living in a lovely four-story waterfront home, although a restful retreat, had begun to be less enjoyable than it had been. However, this restful retreat from Jack's busy law practice involved an hour's commute to and from work. Jack had to leave home before dawn and returned after the sun had set. Instead of week-ends on the boat, we were flying to Cincinnati, Ohio, to visit our grandchildren. Our priorities had changed. Until my accident, those shortcomings had not posed problems for me.

A severe sprain from an accident precipitated 2 years of various surgeries and trying to maneuver through my home on crutches and with a walker. Each

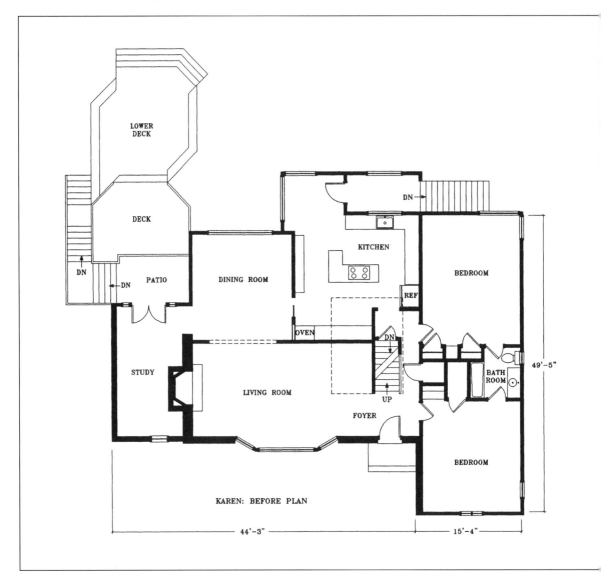

Figure 13-1   Karen and Jack: Before floor plan, with small doorways, cramped bathroom, two steps to the housed front door, and many small rooms and separations.

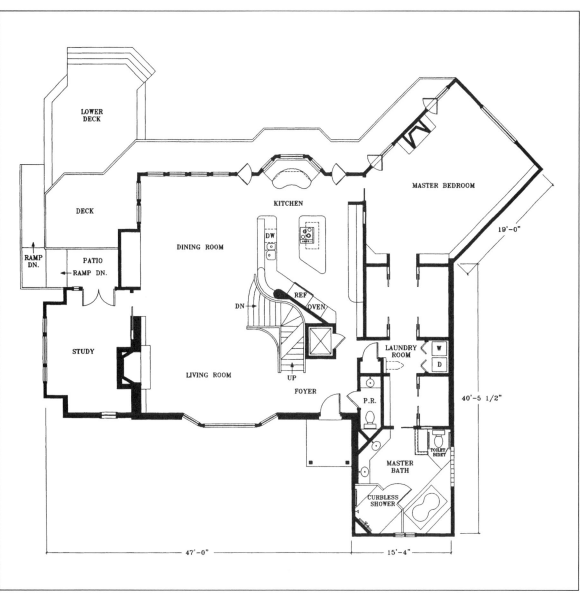

LOWER
DECK

DECK

RAMP
DN.

PATIO

RAMP DN.

STUDY

DINING ROOM

KITCHEN

DW

DN

REF

OVEN

LIVING ROOM

UP

FOYER

MASTER BEDROOM

19'-0"

LAUNDRY
ROOM

W

D

40'-5 1/2"

P.R.

TOILET
BIDET

MASTER
BATH

CURBLESS
SHOWER

47'-0"

15'-4"

Figure 13-2   Karen and Jack: After floor plan.

time the doctors told me to stay off my feet. How do you do that in a four-story home?

The Challenge

One Sunday in Washington, D.C., a Realtor's open house sign caught our eye, and we bought a house designed for one-floor living. It was 15 minutes away from Jack's office, located close to shopping and amenities and nestled in a picturesque community. Of course, the little cottage needed some changes. Built in 1954, it certainly had potential, and I looked forward to creating a home which would allow for my liberation and permit us to age in place.

There were certain musts that I had in mind for this new older home. First, we had to develop a floor plan that would permit us to live on one level adjacent to the street. Second, the home had to be consummately livable and open. All the doorways had to be wide. I was no longer willing to submit myself to battles with narrow spaces. In other words, the laundry basket and I would be able to get through the door at the same time. Abundant, open storage was a must since we are bibliophiles and are passionate about music. We wanted our home to be relaxed and well organized so that movement would be efficient and convenient. This home would need to keep life uncomplicated and safe.

Process and Solutions

I had been intimately involved in the entire design process of this house. The architect, interior designer, and builder were part of the team. It was not surprising how often I had to get them refocused on the basic criterion of functionality. As creative people, they are often beguiled by beauty. I share their love of drama and fantasy, but I am also very practical. It was not always easy to get the team members to remember that if it didn't function as I wanted it to, then the solution was to redesign it. It was a challenge for all of them.

The footprint of the house was altered and several additions were made. An inclined walkway replaced the steps to the front door, which remained where it had been. The staircase was completely demolished, relocated, and replaced by an elegant new stairway leading both to the walk-out basement and upstairs to the guest bedrooms and bath.

The kitchen became the hub of the communal area. It was designed to my specific needs and interests. A stationary table at right angles to the center window with two swivel armchairs opposite each other provides comfort, ease of use, and collegiality. There are no overhead cabinets to obstruct the view; people in one area can see and talk to people in another area. We have an extensive media area which allows television viewing from nearly every part of the open space. Glass walls extend the visual living space to a beautiful garden.

All our new furniture was chosen first for ease in getting in and out of it and for its adaptability and comfort. No longer would I abide by fixtures, furniture, or appliances that pose challenges and hence create anxiety. We kept circulation through and between areas unencumbered. Rather than one large dining table we opted for two square bridge-sized tables for greater flexibility.

In the master bedroom suite, functional ease and access drove decisions. Twin mechanical positioning beds are opposite a fireplace. A pocket door from the kitchen eliminates door-swing problems. From the bed the kitchen breakfast area and gardens are visible. A large-screen television is recessed above the fireplace to allow bedside viewing. Storage is abundant and convenient. Remote controls avoid unnecessary trips to control lights, television, or fireplace. The space is filled with well-lit mini-walk-in closets. Movement sensors turn lights on and off. A second entry from the foyer is located in the center of the corridor opposite a spacious closet containing a washer and dryer.

At the end of the hallway is one of the most joyful but practical and safe bathrooms. This whimsical space would make anyone using it think that they had died and gone to Martha Stewart heaven. Some of the outstanding features that make this a workhorse are as follows:

- A Zoë toilet with a warming seat, a bidet water spray, and an automatic flush

- A half wall that acts as a partition for privacy and has abundant open storage for the occupant's personal hygiene articles

- A large grab bar for assistance on the apron of the storage unit

- A warm-air blower inset into the short side of the partition, cutting down drying time considerably and great for those hard-to-reach areas of the anatomy

A luxurious whirlpool sits in a marble-clad deck. Storage for tub supplies is cleverly housed in cubbies created within the marble side. Also quite unusual is the floor treatment. It is covered with a tightly woven commercial carpet. The toilet area and the shower floor are tile. The transitions between the different finishes have been expertly engineered so that there are no changes in level. The glass-enclosed double shower is as safe as it is luxurious. A curbless transition into the space is welcoming, especially with its two large corner benches which permit seated use. Fixed and adjustable hand-held showerheads permit flexibility of use and allow personal showering preferences. They also make cleanup easier as everything can simply be hosed down. A preset temperature and pressure–balancing valve guarantees that no one will be scalded here. Grab bars are used in various locations inside and outside of the shower.

The sink-vanity areas are higher than usual to cut down on bending while washing. Although these do not permit flexibility in use if either of us should need to use a wheelchair, the oversized laundry closet could easily be fitted with a lower sink for washing. Too often as we age the implements we acquire seem to take over the sink counter. Just think of all the new implements most of us have after 50—a water pick, an interdental flossing machine, a sonic toothbrush. To avoid the unsightly and risky mess of so many appliances and their cords, the cords were shortened. Abundant outlets were placed conveniently around the sink to avoid using adapters at the peril of overloading a circuit. At the touch of a switch the triangulated hydraulically controlled cabinet between the two sinks rises, bringing the appliance out of the lower cabinet in a space that would have been unusable. When not in use, it lowers, leaving a clear counter surface.

Aha!

Our daily living activities have remained the same, but the energy and time it takes to perform them have changed drastically for the better. It may seem an extreme description, but this home represents an absence of trauma. Facing stairs many times a day when I suffer from vertigo slowed me down. I always felt vulnerable. Here, I can manage everything very well. It just seems as though all of the stress is gone.

We have an elevator. Just knowing I have it if I cannot face the stairs is wonderfully reassuring. I can now go grocery shopping whenever I please and bring the groceries to the kitchen by way of the elevator. The little things that I had once been dependent on others to do for me are treasures that add to my life's quality. The elevator also permits us to have older visitors who cannot handle stairs. There are no restrictions for us regarding who can be invited and who cannot. The inclined walkway leading to our front door allows us the pleasure of no stairs, too.

In the other house, I never had the opportunity of seeing Jack in the morning because he rose so early. Now he can leave an hour later. The sleep area of our bedroom, with its wide pocket door, is left open because there are just the two of us. It affords me the joy of making contact with him first thing in the morning and is just one of those unexpected gifts.

We had ultimately retained a driver when the trip from our waterfront home to the city became too difficult for Jack. These days, it is my pleasure to do the chauffeuring. It is part of my personal rehabilitation program. After being an invalid, or treating myself as if I had been one, becoming more active is a joy. Since the inception of this project, I have gotten much of my muscle tone back. The house helps so much.

Living on one level creates peace of mind. Accessibility is everything. All our needs of an intimate nature are just a few steps away through a wide doorway. In a home without barriers, my body is no longer constrained. Most of us adapt to the environments of homes designed without any appreciable thought to human abilities. Our bodies are influenced by space itself. We do not realize how tightly we hold ourselves in until we are in open spaces. Then we are free! It is glorious.

Figure 13-3 Karen and Jack: Front exterior entrance with visitable inclined path.

Figure 13-4 Karen and Jack: Open space in the communal area.

Figure 13-5 Karen and Jack: Bathtub, showing the deck with storage, and camel–and–palm tree tile art.

Figure 13-6 Karen and Jack: Toilet area features wonderful storage and skylights with photosensitive glazing.

Part Three

Professionals' Perspective

This section is presented with information gathered from the designers of each project. In each chapter, designers share their experiences and processes in completing the project being illustrated. Clients are not always aware of the possibilities, but are aware of their needs, and designers have worked not only to create solutions, but to raise awareness.

Introduction by Winthrop Faulkner, AIA

MY GRANDMOTHER, WHO WAS A CLIENT AND FRIEND OF FRANK LLOYD WRIGHT, USED TO quote the brilliant architect's adage: "Give me the luxuries of life and I will find a way to get along, without the bare necessities." Wright was referring to his inability to resist the purchase of a carpet, cape, automobile, Japanese print, or other temptation, regardless of cost, if it met his very high standards of taste. And, to Mr. Wright, the bare necessities may have had a different meaning than simple food and shelter.

Having designed and built houses in many parts of this country and abroad for the past 30 years, I have gradually developed an awareness of another form of bare necessity. This one is related to the way we and our fellow human beings live or wish to live, in comfort rather than in luxury. One can, of course, do both. I refer to the comfort of accessibility, which is addressed in what has now become a familiar term: *universal design*. Making buildings, particularly our homes, accessible, comfortable, and safe for children, the middle aged, and the elderly, all of whom may have different physical requirements, means adopting universal design measures. How to do this imaginatively and almost invisibly is the challenge to the architect, the designer, and the recipient. There is an obligation not only to solve the access problem functionally and efficiently but so subtly that one is barely aware of the ramp, elevator, plumbing fixture, hand rail, garden path, or lamp that has been incorporated to make everyone more comfortable.

When I get together with my clients to discuss their programmatic requirements for a new house, I try to do more listening than talking. People's ability to clearly express their functional and aesthetic needs varies tremendously. Some can say in a few minutes what others cannot define in a day. Design professionals must absorb the words and feelings of a client whether clearly stated or not. There should be a detailed building program, or wish list, and it should include information about the unique needs of the owner, both those that are apparent and those that are not.

Like the critical issue of energy conservation, universal design should be a prime consideration when buying or building a new house. I do not know how many of us in the design and construction field in America are paying attention to the urgent needs of access for the future. I suspect it is not encouraging. Most building standards required by the Americans with Disabilities Act are at the moment largely directed at commercial construction. Home building needs a nudge. When residential design becomes universal, we will all be better off.

Chapter 14

Bare Necessities

CLIENT: Lucy
ARCHITECT: Winthrop Faulkner
PHOTOGRAPHER: Norman McGrath

IN THE EARLY 1990S, I WAS ASKED TO DESIGN A LARGE HOUSE IN WESTCHESTER County, New York, by a psychiatrist whose specialty is counseling individuals of all ages who use wheelchairs. She insisted that the house must be fully accessible to patients and friends. As we designed the house together we made sure literally at every turn that the wheelchair and occupant could go everywhere. The surprise feature of the house is a music and meditation room, a cozy hideaway, which is built into the roof and has spectacular views of the Hudson River. It is accessible by a circular stair, but also by an elevator behind a paneled door to the left of the fireplace. What a pity if we had not made this, the most dramatic and serene room, accessible to all.

Stairs leading to a sumptuous landing bring attention and presence to the home's entry. Perhaps the expression of this home's facade could not have been achieved without the stairs, as level changes do create drama. It would be foolhardy to envision that in a perfect world all homes would have entryways on grade. In this design, alternatives were also incorporated. An inclined walk leads to the south terrace and lily pond. It provides an accessible route and entry to

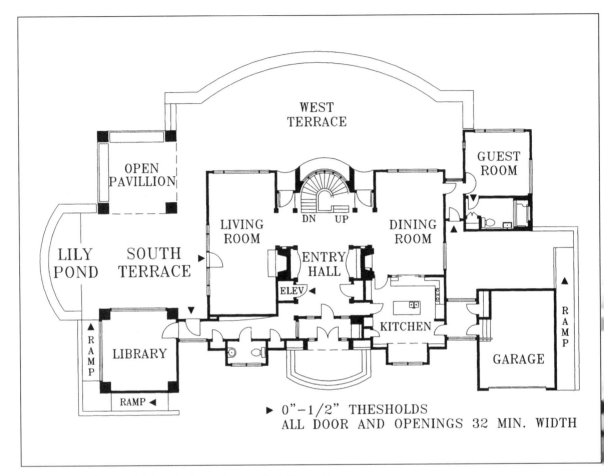

Figure 14-1 Faulkner Project: Main floor plan.

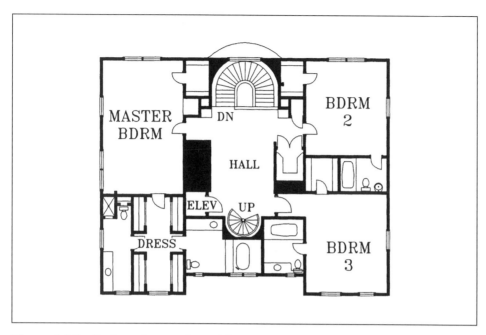

Figure 14-2 Faulkner Project: Second floor plan.

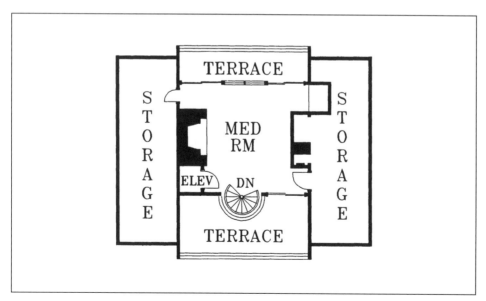

Figure 14-3 Faulkner Project: Loft plan.

either the living room or the corridor that leads to the library or entry hall. All thresholds within and without are 0 to ½ in, making transitions possible for persons with assistive devices.

The staircase of the reception gallery is the focal point. In addition to the drama of the stairs, an elevator provides another means of vertical access within the house. Given the soaring ceiling and the increased distance between floors, the option might be anyone's choice. Minding the prevailing symmetry, the elevator was located opposite a guest coat closet. All doors and openings have been kept to a minimum of 32 in wide. Again, threshold heights are a maximum of ½ in. This is a home that is welcome to all. This is also a home in which one can age in place.

The theme of "Welcome to all" is continued in the bathrooms. Since the house is large and the guest room wing is on the first floor, there was room for a conventional powder room off the reception gallery plus a guest bathroom. In the guest bath, it was simple to include a roll-in shower, adjustable-height sink insulated from below, lever-handle faucets, and a toilet equipped with grab bars. This room is attractive and accessible to all guests. The richness of materials selected for this space ensure not only function, but also a high aesthetic.

Figure 14-4 Faulkner Project: Antefoyer features low-maintenance solar materials and provides a thermal barrier without need for level changes.

Figure 14-5 Faulkner Project: View to the dining room showing carpet sculpted to minimize level changes.

Figure 14-6   Faulkner Project: Library features natural materials, accessible window-opening hardware, sensible furniture arrangement, and chairs appropriate for a variety of uses.

Figure 14-7   Faulkner Project: Reception gallery.

Figure 14-8   Faulkner Project: Loft with elevator.

Chapter 15

Real Life Design

CLIENT: GE Appliances

DESIGNER: Mary Jo Peterson, CKD, CBD, CHE

PHOTOGRAPHY: Property of General Electric

As a kitchen and bath designer, I have worked with individuals whose size, shape, and physical abilities helped to create the parameters of the job. In each, the design solution brought me tremendous personal rewards as I experienced a client's success in a newly supportive environment. In this case, my client was General Electric, a major appliance manufacturer, and its customers, and the focus shifted. At first, I felt that my work was being somewhat compromised as I weighed designing for access for a person with a particular disability against what could be marketed to the masses. Eventually, I came to appreciate the true meaning and value of universal design. Now I was designing not in response to one household's specific needs, but with the challenge of creating a kitchen that could be flexible, a kitchen that would support most people most of the time— in other words, a truly universal kitchen. Add to this that the bulk of the consumers of my work in this project would be builders, remodelers, and end users of production and custom homes. This required that I work with moderately priced materials and products, using them in nontraditional ways that would be aesthetically appealing and accessible. Instead of improving the lives of one

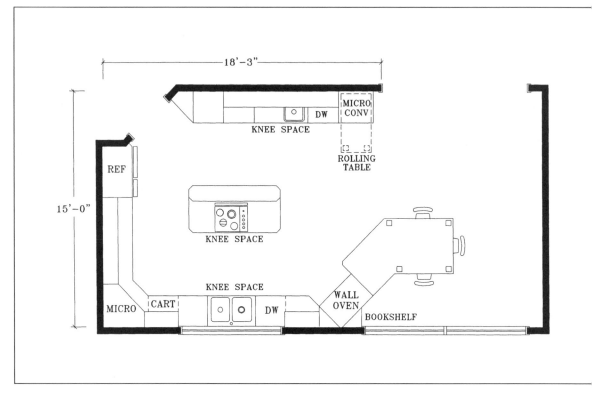

Figure 15-1 Peterson project: The GE Real Life Design Kitchen.

household's members, I might help to change many households' options. It was and continues to be an amazing opportunity to contribute to the way we live in our homes.

The family that I created, and for whom this kitchen was designed, includes five members. They are a couple in their forties, both working; a very tall teenage son; a 7-year-old daughter; and one grandparent, whose age has brought some changes in physical ability. Grandma sometimes uses a mobility aid and has some arthritis, changing vision, and some hearing and memory loss. Mom also finds herself forgetful at times, and is experiencing some of the arthritis that her mother has. Teenage son does everything at triple speed, and 7-year-old daughter has a shorter attention span and somewhat less balance and dexterity than she will one day have. While Mom and Dad are off to work and son is at basketball practice, Grandma and granddaughter are often looking after each other. Everyone in the family helps in the kitchen and congregates there to catch up with each other.

The design challenge was to create a kitchen that would support this variety of activities and of people, respectful of their varying sizes, shapes, and abilities. This space must feel and look like the heart of the home that it is, and it must fall within reasonable parameters of size and cost.

The solution is a kitchen that responds to the way we live today. The main work pattern moves from the refrigerator through a preparation area to the main sink and dishwasher, on to the oven or across to the island cooktop. The secondary work pattern moves from the refrigerator to the secondary sink and dishwasher and on to the microwave-convection oven. The layout allows for multiple cooks and a variety of activities taking place simultaneously, or for one cook to concentrate efforts in a smaller area.

In the main work area, a side-by-side refrigerator with pass-through handles and an in-door dispenser of ice and water provides storage at varied heights. With a 36-in-high counter, pull-outs provide lowered work surfaces for shorter or seated cooks. A step stool folds out of the corner to provide better access to open-shelf wall cabinets. The open shelves provide easy recall of stored items. In other wall cabinets, a pull-down mechanism improves safe access to upper shelves. Beyond the traditional drawers and roll-out shelves, a corner recycling bin is designed for easy emptying. The corner microwave at counter height is within most everyone's reach and view, and it provides for minimal transfer. A rolling cart provides further assistance for moving items around the kitchen. This cart has a heatproof surface and is curbed on three sides to support safe and easy transfer of hot items.

The main sink is height adjustable, allowing for comfortable use by most people, from seated or shorter cooks, to taller reluctant cleanup crew members. The space below the sink is covered by a removable panel that allows access to plumbing when needed and provides protection between the plumbing and seated or shorter cooks, all coordinated in finish with the cabinetry. A large window brings in natural light, and flanking wall cabinets are accessorized to bring storage within the reach of more cooks. The oven is placed at a height that allows for less bending and shorter transfer distance. The adjacent built-in table serves as a seated prep area, a dining table or desk, and a transition into the family room.

The island cooking center includes a smooth surface for easy transfer, storage at the point of use, and a downdraft venting system with controls within most cooks' reach. Bifold doors below the cooktop allow full use of the area for storage or seating. The back of the island is elevated to 45 in, providing a raised working area. It also creates a visual and physical boundary or backsplash for the cooking area.

The second work pattern, geared more to the shorter or seated cook, moves from the refrigerator past the back of the island, where wall cabinets built on 9-in-high toekicks provide storage within easy reach. The plate rack and pantry offer additional accessible storage. The sink has been set to one side of the 30-in-high counter to provide the greatest stretch of work area, with the faucet and instant hot-water dispenser set to one side for easier access. Most storage above the universal reach range (15 to 48" above finished floor [AFF]) is used for display. Adjacent pull-outs provide additional counters at 30" AFF, including one with a cutout to grip a bowl and free up one of the cook's hands. The dishwasher here is elevated, providing better access for most and easy transfer to dish storage immediately across from it. The microwave-convection oven has a door that drops down close to table height, again minimizing transfer. The movable table below it provides additional seated work surface. When needed, it can be moved to add to the seating at the built-in table. A smaller rolling cart again helps in transfer of items around the kitchen.

Finishes in the kitchen are low-glare and contrast is used judiciously for accent and function. Counters have some light and some dark areas for working with dark or light ingredients. They have a high-contrast raised edge to serve as a visual and tactile guide. Again, contrast in the flooring is used as accent and to assist in wayfinding. Dark faucets are set in light counters, dark appliances in light cabinetry. Lighting is plentiful and adjustable.

The overall character of this kitchen is open and friendly. Wide work aisles invite multiple cooks and respect cooks using mobility aids. Display areas allow for personalization and limit the need to store frequently used items out of the cooks' reach. Generous light and accents of color add warmth and improve visibility. Changes in counter surfaces add personality and improve function, as with the heatproof tiles used near cooking appliances.

While the goal of this project was to provide a source of ideas and information for others, it continues to be a great source of learning for me. Based on information and experience with clients of varying sizes and abilities, I planned many things into the kitchen that seem to work well and some things that I have since learned to improve. A benefit of the kitchen is that it can be seen and tried by so many different people, and from each I learn where the design of space and products can change. A key to successful universal design is to ask the end user what is needed, then to listen, then to design not based on personal perceptions, but on what has been said. From a person with visual impairments, I learned that the tactile counter edge was an aid in wayfinding, but that the traditional red color indicating *on* or *hot* on the cooktop could not be easily seen against the black cooktop. I learned that there is a critical balance between a comfortable height for the oven door and a height that puts the controls out of reach. I learned that many people using wheelchairs use a parallel approach to the oven, and that an angled corner microwave oven at counter height is not within reach of a cook using a wheelchair unless there is a knee space below. I learned that by improving access to the upper sections of wall cabinets, a cook might be more willing to give up enough base-cabinet storage to create knee space. My own eyes taught me that although rolling carts add tremendous flexibility in the kitchen, I can get carried away, as I did with the smaller cart that resembles a space module more than an integral part of the kitchen.

On the other hand, the kitchen has never been met with anything but enthusiasm from people of every age, size, ability, and disability. Specifically, people who are taller than average (whatever that is), appreciate the adjustable-height sink, as it allows them a comfortable height at which to work. Adjusting the height of the oven and the dishwasher brought positive comments from everyone, as it cuts down on bending and reaching. The teenage son in our family can now help clean and cook at a sink that fits his height. The use of bifold doors under the cooktop reinforced a concern I had about knee spaces. Where retractable doors would take up as much as 6 in of the knee space width when open, the bifold doors take none. The added clearance for a person using a wheelchair makes the approach much easier. Imagine being in a hurry and driving your car into a garage that's an exact fit. That extra space matters.

Like the previous examples and true to its definition, universal design in this kitchen has advantages for many people. The greater number of drawers instead of doors eliminates one step in the access process, which brings comments from cooks using mobility aids, those having reduced control of their hands, people working in smaller spaces, people with low vision or memory loss, and people who want a more efficient kitchen.

The lever faucet helps when hands are dirty from gardening or the garage, when they're full, perhaps of an infant who needs a face wash, or when the cook has a disability that impacts the use of his or her hands. The rolling cart makes it easier to transport things through the kitchen, whether for several bags of groceries, the Thanksgiving turkey, or for younger or older hands to transport dishes to the table.

The Real Life Design Kitchen has been a wonderful tool, not just as a source of ideas, but more as a demonstration of universal design as an attractive, functional, marketable response to what we all want from our kitchens today. It has been a step on the bridge between those of us who embrace universal design and the rest of the architects, designers, builders, remodelers, and consumers who are growing in awareness and understanding. It now has a permanent home at Virginia Technical Institute in Virginia, where it will continue to educate people and build bridges. I am grateful for the part I have played in its evolution.

Figure 15-2 Peterson project: The GE Real Life Design Kitchen.

Figure 15-3 Peterson project: Refrigerator and open shelves; note open storage and varied counter heights.

Figure 15-4 Peterson project: Island and knee space features heatproof surface and smooth-surface cooktop with side controls.

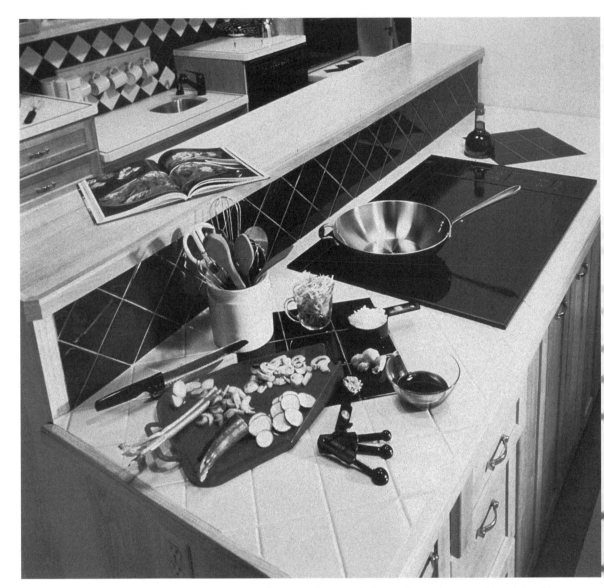

Figure 15-5 Peterson project: Contrast for visual clarity shown by movable table, elevated dishwasher, varied counter heights including pull-out work surfaces, and display area.

Figure 15-6 Peterson project: Second work center.

Chapter 16

On the Street Where You Live

DESIGNERS: The Washington, D.C., Chapter of the International Furnishings and
Design Association (IFDA); Ina Mae Kaplan, FIFDA, ASID;
Donna Ralston-Latham, FIFDA, ASID; and Irma Laufer Dobkin, ASID, FIFDA

ARCHITECT: Laurence A. Frank

WE WOULD LIKE TO SHARE THE STORY OF AN ACCOMPLISHED JOURNEY. IT IS THE transformation of a simple ranch house on a peaceful suburban street into a shared group home for three clients with various limitations. This community venture was an unusual collaboration between the members of the Washington Chapter of the International Furnishings and Design Association (IFDA), the Lt. Joseph P. Kennedy Institute for the Developmentally Challenged (Kennedy Institute), and the U.S. Department of Housing and Urban Development (HUD).

When the Kennedy Institute was awarded a foundation grant from HUD to procure 4 additional houses to add to its 16 established homes, it approached its long-term friends at IFDA to request designer leftovers to try to fill these homes.

Members of our chapter wanted this project to be a laboratory where they could explore and apply the principles of universal design and access. Dr. Birkel, principal of the Kennedy Institute, was interested in developing a model where residents, ill or frail, could remain in the group setting and age in place. In addition, the institute wanted to explore the impact that a sup-

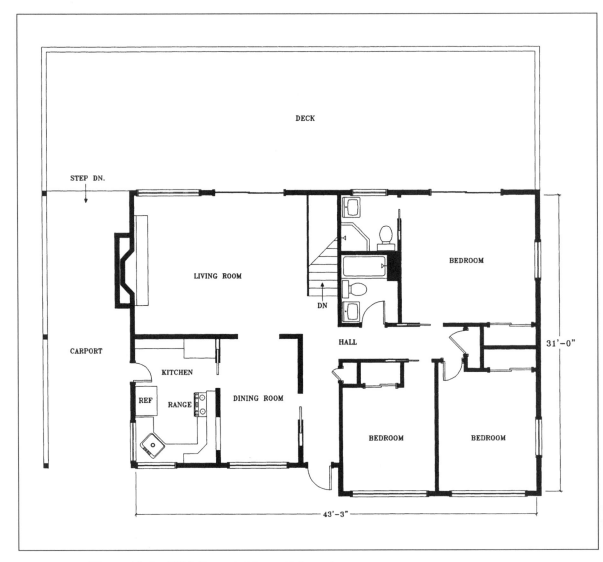

Figure 16-1 IFDA Kennedy House: Before plan.

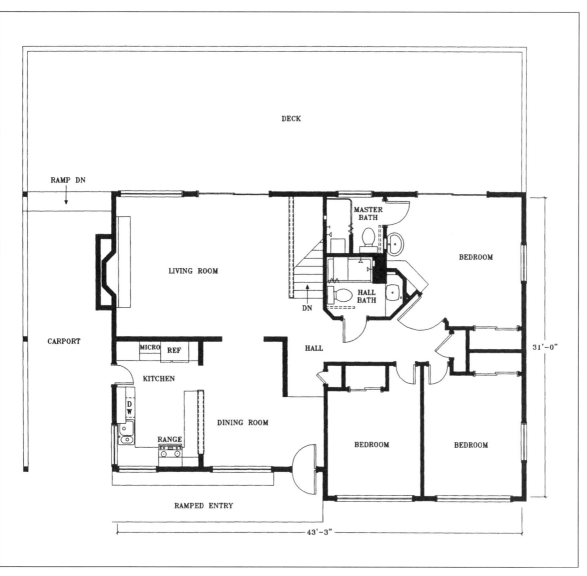

Figure 16-2   IFDA Kennedy House: After plan.

portive environment might have on staff morale. Turnover among care providers is endemic in most group homes. Traditionally, most group homes focus solely on the residents' needs to the exclusion of those of the staff. Finally, the institute wanted to have a welcoming and functional area for home staff meetings.

The Event Committee addressed the design challenge. Our objectives were the following:

1. Create a comfortable, safe, accessible, and attractive home adapted to the tastes and requirements of three individuals with specific disabilities— Fred, Chuck, and Michael—and their caregivers.

2. Enable the men to entertain family and friends.

3. Enable the residents to age in place.

This was all to be accomplished by contributions, donations, and volunteers and without monetary impact to the chapter. As with all clients, each of the men was interviewed with his care providers to determine their functional and aesthetic needs. Not only diversity of abilities but diversity of spirit was respected. With the program requirements defined, the problem solving began. First, the main circulation areas required evaluation. On the main level, the foyer to the bedroom area was too narrow to permit ease of movement, particularly with an assistive device. Although a bearing wall had to be moved at significant expense, a wider hall was pivotal to the development of a universally designed space. Basically, we removed all unnecessary partitions, preferring to develop specific function areas within a larger open space. Not only did this improve circulation, but it also improved the ambiance of the entire house.

On review with HUD this home was identified as a single-family dwelling, and as such it did not have to comply with the letter of the law. The bath in the bedroom was made fully accessible rather than the hall bath. The living room was left pretty much intact. It needed little change beyond furnishings. A 42-in-high wall replaced an ineffective wrought-iron railing for safety reasons. The selection of furniture had three layout objectives:

1. Allow for the physical differences created by people's different heights.

2. Arrange the furniture to allow a seated user to pull up to either area of the living room without moving any of the permanent pieces.

3. Keep the direct route to the deck unobstructed.

We worked to achieve each while maintaining full visual access to the wonderfully large deck.

The original house had many small, compartmentalized rooms. The kitchen would permit only one cook. A wheelchair could not fit nor be manipulated in it. The entrance to the dining area from the kitchen had been narrow. A very small pocket door from the original entry hall would also limit access. The shared hall bath was made larger, resulting in a safer, more comfortable area. It has a higher than normal sink because the additional height affords benefits. Standing users can more easily lean on the counter to wash. The hand spray permits hair washing should full bathing be difficult.

"One size does not fit all" is the axiom of universal design. We were designing for a variety of people with a continuum of needs. The former master bedroom, which was significantly larger than the others, was made smaller to permit an ample turnaround area at the end of the widened hallway. Additional space was annexed for the shared bath's double sink area. The approaches to each bedroom had been very congested. The 5-ft turnaround space provides easier access to each bedroom.

Although the bedrooms were rather small, the design teams developed responsive and imaginative solutions that reflect the personalities of their occupants. To support the chores the men do independently, such as making beds and tidying up, access around the beds was well planned, as were the systems for the storage and retrieval of clothing. Each of the men has collections that require space. Michael's enormous sock collection found a home in the drawers beneath his boat-shaped bed. A large unobstructed work area in Fred's room supports his love of puzzles and hooking rugs. Chuck's Elvis memorabilia collection, substantial stereo components, and related musical collections were housed in a custom-designed storage-display built-in which also serves as the landing surface for his wall-hung sink. Each bedroom reflects a personal preference. Michael's is the seashore, Fred's is vivid floral puzzles and rugs, and Chuck's is Elvis—complete with a custom headboard that is a replica of Elvis's pink Cadillac.

We redeveloped the entrances into and out of the house. The front steps were eliminated and replaced with an inclined walk terminating in an ample landing level with the front door. Rather than a ramp, which is a dead giveaway that someone handicapped lives here, we elected to relandscape and incorporate the inclined walk. The aesthetics of the solution were carefully considered bearing not only on resale value but also on the homeowner's ability to thoroughly enjoy living in a home that has no barriers.

Figure 16-3 IFDA Kennedy House: Kitchen features combined open kitchen and dining area, large tactile phone, and generous and accessible storage and work areas.

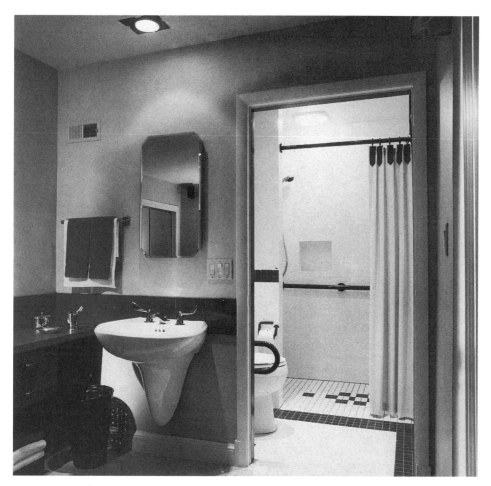

Figure 16-4 IFDA Kennedy House: Chuck's bath features fold-down support arm, curb-less shower, and vanity sink in bedroom area.

Figure 16-5 IFDA Kennedy House: Hall bath features shallow tub, fold-down tub seat, high toilet, fold-down support arm, and transom.

Chapter 17

Lifespan Design

DESIGNER: Judith R. Bracht, CKD, CBD, IFDA

ARCHITECT: Carl Neuberg, AIA

THE GENERATION THAT ONCE DIDN'T TRUST ANYONE OVER 30, VIEWED 40 AS TRAU-matic, and 50 as unthinkable is finally approaching that unthinkable milestone.

Over the last few years many more clients have been requesting luxury bath-rooms and kitchens. Although none of them outright discuss the need for safety per se or talk about the changes in their ability as they age, the accouterments that they want in these rooms nevertheless underscore their realization that more thoughtfully designed spaces can make aging less formidable. As a designer I have become quite adept at designing universally without all the accompanying discourse which, for some reason, they do not want to hear or discuss. Yet, when presented in terms of individualizing a design solution to meet their unique desires for a more convenient and gracious lifestyle, both the client and the designer achieve a universal end that is satisfying to both. Typical of these clients are Jill and Larry.

It is telling that Jill and Larry made no mention of a safely designed bath-room or plans to accommodate their later years. Instead, he wanted the luxury

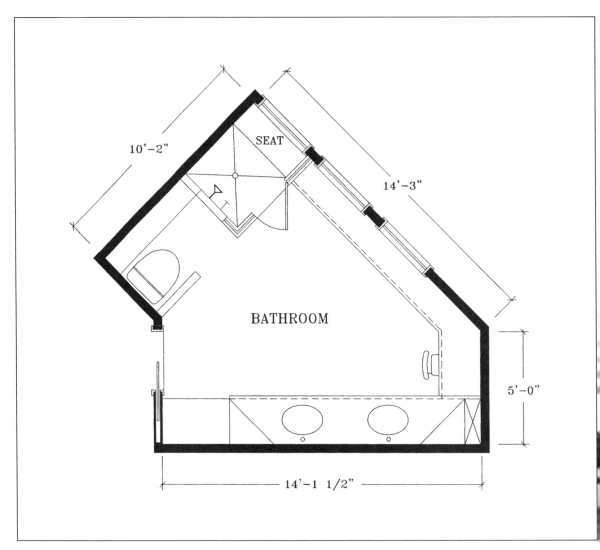

Figure 17-1 Bracht project: Floor plan with pocket door, storage at point of use, and removable partition to toilet area.

found throughout a lifetime of travel to first-class hotels in his own bathroom. His reluctance to discuss aging is common.

Jill and Larry have lived in their home for a number of years and have raised two children in it. Their home is ideally located on the shore of a suburban lake, surrounded by beautiful landscaping that creates an idyllic setting. As an empty-nest family their needs had changed. To meet their current lifestyle requirements as well as the anticipated requirements for their golden years, they decided to build an addition. The area of the home that initially had three bedrooms was transformed into a generous master suite consisting of two dressing areas, a private study, and the new enlarged bathroom and sleeping area.

"Jill and I had been tripping over each other for years," says Larry of the bathroom he and his wife shared in their 44-year-old home. So when they launched this project, he knew just what needed to be done. A frequent business traveler, Larry wanted the new bath to have the kinds of luxurious amenities he had found in some of the nation's best hotels. "I came to appreciate the elegance of really beautiful materials and the openness and spaciousness of hotel baths," he says. Their new bath, the result of collaboration between their architect and me, certainly fulfills those expectations. At roughly 14 by 17 ft, the delta-shaped room provides the capaciousness they craved. Mirror-lined walls, a 4- by 4-ft skylight and a frameless, glass-enclosed shower play up the room's open character. More than 24 linear feet of polyester-finished cabinetry—suspended above the floor and topped with slab granite—incorporates abundant storage plus a built-in makeup table and two widely separated sinks. The floor's distinctive 12- by 12-in granite tile extends into the shower, where it is scored for traction. The shower is curbless. Larry had grown tired of stepping over the side of a bathtub to take a shower.

Safety features became as important as the aesthetic application. Rather than safety, however, these features were perceived as conveniences to make life better. Included on their must have list was a toilet compartment with a high-seated water closet. The area had to have a telephone and storage conveniently nearby.

The shower area was designed with a number of features to enhance safety while preserving a luxury feel. The beautiful granite slab in the shower creates a play on pattern and scale. A seat and hand-held shower promotes safer, easier washing. Individual pressure-balanced valves with blade handles (or levers, which are easier to turn than knobs) for the shower head and hand shower reduce the risk of scalding. The glass shower door opens outward into the room in case someone inside should need assistance.

The vanity area also became a special element of the overall design. Jill wanted a seated makeup area with a pull-out makeup light and a magnifying mirror. The vanities were placed at an adult height of 36 in to reduce lower back stress. Towel bars were placed conveniently below the lavatory. The storage below the sinks was recessed, making access a bit inconvenient, but it does conceal the plumbing pipes. An added benefit is that a seated user can pull up to the sink and not have a flush cabinet blocking knee access. Linen storage, drawers for lingerie, toiletries, and a laundry hamper were also provided. In the toileting area, the privacy wall has been built for easy removal, should that become desirable for improved access. The flooring runs under the wall, so the floor tiles immediately under it could be replaced if it is removed.

The lighting is dramatic and beautiful both during the day and night. The glass-block wall and skylight provide privacy, but allow diffused natural light to drift into the space. During the evening, the dimmable under-cabinet halogen lights provide ambiance. The extensive use of granite, combined with the polyester finish on the cabinetry and the reflection of all the mirrors, create the richness and drama that my clients had envisioned.

Many people realize that they need these features after taking care of elderly parents. They begin to understand that what they have now just isn't enough. After experiences with manipulating parents into showers, adjusting temperatures, and getting drenched by wall-mounted showerheads, these adult child caregivers decide to redesign for the future. Now 90 percent of the bathrooms I design include hand-held showers, the 3-ft-high vanity, and, of course and most certainly, grab bars. These three items should be in every home, no matter the age of the home or the homeowner. These items make the bathroom universal—designed to be available and accessible to the least able user, but generally beneficial to every user.

Figure 17-2   Bracht project: Vanities and seated makeup area features recessed marble toekick, generous storage, recessed vanity cabinet doors, and towel bars below the vanity sinks.

Figure 17-3 Bracht project: The curbless shower features fixed and hand-held shower heads, grab bars, and a door that swings either way.

Chapter 18

For Today, Tomorrow, and Always

CLIENT: DeLaura Custom Builders
DESIGNER: Jean DeLaura, ASID
PHOTOGRAPHY: Property of Design One

As an interior designer and model merchandiser in the greater Chicago area, Jean DeLaura looked for an avenue to develop and promote universal design. When her husband Dennis, a custom home builder, took on a development involving infill within the City of Chicago, Jean went to work and the result is the Jesse Owens, "a unique universally designed home for today's city-life households."

The obvious goal of this project was to design a home that would meet the needs of its owner throughout life, responding to the desire to age in place. The job site dictated that this would have to be done in a two-story house, no wider than 19 ft on a lot 30 ft wide, and it would need to be done at competitive price levels.

A less obvious, but equally important goal for Jean was to impact the way the housing industry looks at universal design and home building. She sought to demonstrate that a home could be "accessible, adaptable, affordable, and attractive."

A review of the plan reveals essential living and entertaining spaces and a master suite on the main floor, with additional sleeping space on the second

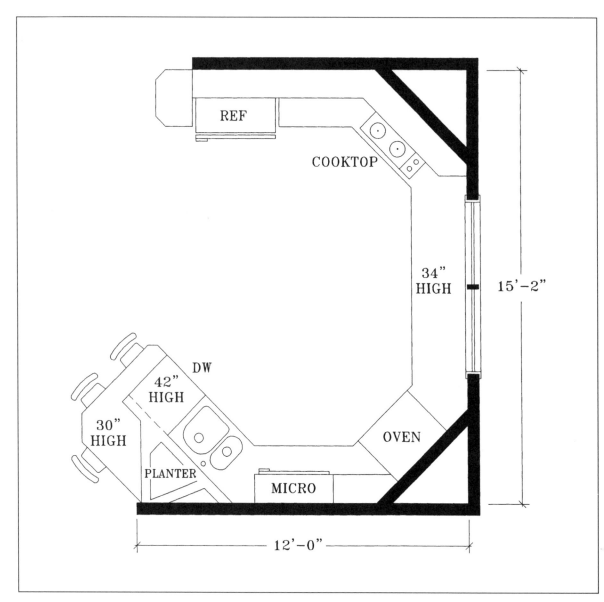

Figure 18-1 DeLaura project: First floor plan.

floor. The linear design, necessitated by the narrowness of the lot and home, lends itself to easier maneuvering spaces. Stairs were oversized for easier stepping. Outside, the typical six steps up to the entry were cut to two, and a convenience ramp was created to access the side entry. A full basement housed utilities.

Throughout the plan, hallways were eliminated or maintained a minimum 42-in width. Doors provided a minimum clear width of 32 in. There were no level changes on the main floor, and thresholds were eliminated or kept to a minimum. Handrails were installed on all ramps and stairways, and reinforcement was built into walls where additional rails might be desired. Lever handles were used throughout. Outlets and switches were brought within the universal range.

A variation on a U-shape, the kitchen allows ease of maneuvering and limited need for transfer of items because they can be moved along the continuous counter. The high contrast adds drama and supports visual wayfinding. The increased height of the toekicks and decreased depths of the lower portion of the base cabinets truly follows the contours of a person using a wheelchair. Access to storage is improved through the installation of roll-out shelves in the pantry and in all base cabinets. The kitchen includes several counter heights, and appliances were selected and installed for improved access.

As the model was sold and the project wound down, Jean reflected on her experiences with insights that might help any of us. When asked what she might change, Jean mentioned the delicate balance between added cost and desired features. Although she had considered bringing the furnace to the main floor for improved access, it remained in the basement as a savings of cost and space. Jean opted for a powder room, knowing that the space would be an ideal location for an elevator, and she continues to ponder that decision. There were some hidden costs for the changes, such as the added cost for excavation to a two-step entry over the original six steps. Added costs for universal access were estimated at $20,000 on a $240,000 home. Once on the market, the house sold in 6 months, which would suggest that the design decisions Jean made were good ones.

When asked what the most difficult aspect of this project was, Jean first responded with the challenges of squeezing everything into a 30-ft lot and meeting codes and Chicago's guidelines for the style of a home. On further thought, she cited working with the trades to do nontraditional things. Even with a startup meeting and plan reviews, she had to check daily and sometimes had to require that things be redone, not according to tradition, but according to the plans. It is human nature that old habits die hard.

The Jesse Owens won awards in the Chicago area and nationally. The message it sends, according to Jean, is that "builders need to reexamine the way we use our homes and to make new homes more functional for the life of the homeowner." No matter what price range, more access must be included and marketed.

As to marketing, the message must be *better design* more than *barrier-free* or *accessible*. As an example, master suites lend themselves to universal design and are marketed as luxury, not access, although they can be both. After all, this home was universally designed, or designed for anyone, and an able-bodied couple bought it after a short time on the market. If done well, universal design is what it sets out to be—universal in its aesthetics and its function.

Figure 18-2   DeLaura project: The Jesse Owens kitchen.

Figure 18-3 DeLaura project: Appliances were chosen for best access, including side-swing-door oven.

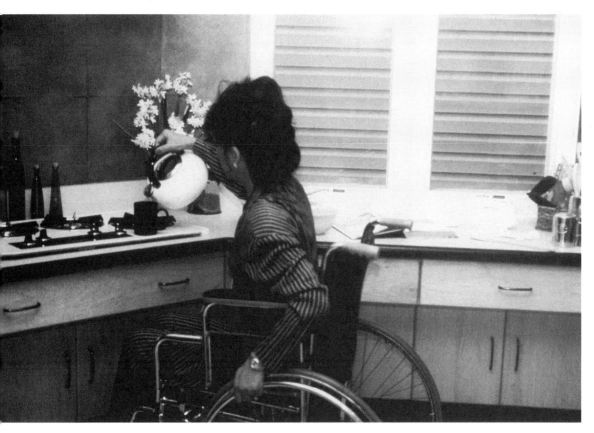

Figure 18-4   DeLaura project: Flexibility allows kitchen to function for seated or standing cooks.

Chapter 19

The Living Center

CLIENT: GE Appliances

DESIGNER: Mary Jo Peterson, CKD, CBD, CHE

PHOTOGRAPHY: Property of General Electric

AS WITH THE REAL LIFE DESIGN KITCHEN, MY CLIENT FOR THE LIVING CENTER WAS General Electric. Having received a tremendously positive response, the goal this time was to take it a step further. This kitchen was to be a living center, with kitchen and clothing care open to the family room. Responding to the growing trend toward a space where everyone and anyone gathers for function and fun, this was to be the place for cooking, dining, computing, doing laundry, watching television, pursuing hobbies, sharing time with family, and entertaining friends. In other words, this was to be a truly universal space—flexible, accessible, and adaptable to different people and different activities. It was to be finished affordably and appropriately so that each area would complement the others. Again, the target was designers, builders, remodelers, and consumers.

The result in this case is a fluid space, unified by design elements and more by the interrelationships of people and activities. The flexibility that supports people of diverse sizes and abilities also supports varied activities. At one point in the day, a lowered work surface adjacent to the oven may serve as a baking center or a place for a seated or shorter cook to work comfortably. Later, the same space

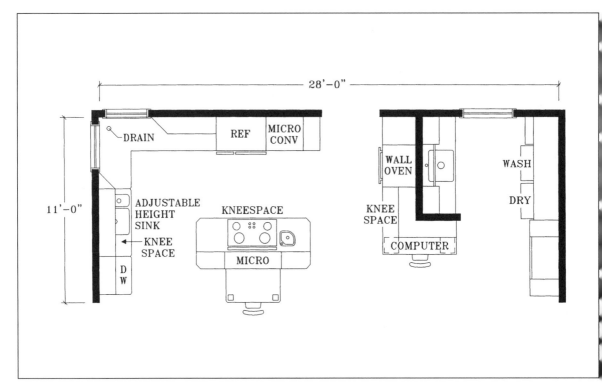

Figure 19-1 Peterson project: The GE Living Center plan.

may work with the computer center around the corner, so that two people might do homework or pay bills. Should there be three people who wish to sit to work, the adjacent cart can be rolled out to offer a third seated work area. The dining table has casters concealed within two legs for easy movement and stability when in place, so it might easily be moved to the computer area for more workspace.

Another example is the sink, which can be lowered to a comfortable and functional height for a seated or shorter cook and can also be raised to a comfortable height for a 6 ft 6 in cleanup crew member. The open storage system that stores linens from the adjacent clothing-care center can be adjusted in height to be a work surface with storage and lighting for craft work or other personal interests.

The 12-in cabinet that stores computer disks can be pivoted out of the way to access the central processor or to allow Junior to sit adjacent to Dad at the computer for tutoring.

Who doesn't benefit from easier access? Although the actual work space of this kitchen is fairly concentrated, there are five places where a person can sit to cook if desired. For those of us who prefer to concentrate our tasks in one area, the island cooktop and adjacent sink would be one spot. With the sink so close, a cook can fill and empty a pot with very little need to lift or transfer. Another cook might work from the refrigerator to the main sink, an area full of easily accessed storage and work surfaces at several heights. A third cook might move around to the table, using the second microwave as needed. Beyond the usual accessories that improve access, the backsplash railing system increases flexible storage at point of use and within the universal reach range (15 to 48 in).

The typical empty space behind a corner cabinet houses a drain so that herbs hung in the corner window area can easily be cared for and watered. The success of this area is enhanced by both natural and grow lights and the in-counter compost station between the corner and the main sink.

Fit and finish of details in this space were carefully considered in an effort to showcase ideas that builders and remodelers could see, understand, and repeat. The interesting twist here is that universal design details enhance the aesthetics of the space, a far cry from the typical concern that universal design must translate to a "handicap kitchen" look. The dishwasher is elevated, with a wall cabinet dropped onto the counter above it, improving access to both. The difference in height between the dishwasher and the adjacent space is appealing, as it creates a visual barrier between the sink and food-prep mess and the family room without a full wall or a tall unit that might create a blocked feeling. Glass in both front and side panels on the wall cabinet and a lighted interior with glass shelves further open the space and create a transition from the preparation area to the adjoining family room space. Combined with the shallow drawers in the lower section of the wall cabinet, the effect is furniturelike and puts tableware at its point of use. Next to the refrigerator, there is a tall, shallow cabinet with an inverted face frame and glass upper doors and side panel. As it is installed, sideways, it is again an aesthetic improvement over the enclosed feeling of the typical entry area, and it creates easily accessed visible storage within the reach of most cooks. Decorative pendants accent the room and add light at the island work surface. Again, these examples are noteworthy because they are basic universal design concepts that demonstrate improved aesthetics.

Working within the parameters of a builder or a remodeler, this design has to maintain a delicate balance. For the most part, a moderate budget was maintained, with midrange materials used. The cabinets are semi-custom-manufactured cabinets with several areas built of stock parts and pieces on the job. The counters are solid surface veneer and tile with glass tile inlays. The floor is vinyl sheet goods with a custom pattern.

These are examples of how standard, traditional products and materials can be designed into a space in less traditional ways, making them more attractive and universal and keeping costs down. In addition, the concepts previously discussed—improved flexibility, access, and function—are aspects builders and remodelers know they can sell and that consumers want and will pay for. These are the features emphasized in marketing universal design successfully, not access based on specific abilities, but the resulting improvement in function appeals to all.

In an ideal world, every space and product would be supportive of each of us, regardless of our differences. In reality, "One size does not fit all," as the saying goes, and there are aspects of this design that will not work for everyone all the time. However, among the work stations there are spaces that support similar activities by cooks of most any stature, age, or ability.

While each project we design has its own parameters and each client has his or her own preferences, I have enjoyed my part in this example of a broader interpretation of universal design, not just for differences in people, but also for differences in lifestyle. It has been a wonderful opportunity to work with product designers and suppliers, to say, "I wish I could . . ." and have their assistance in pushing the envelope on their products. This team effort is part of the marketing needed if universal design is to reach the general public. When we succeed in this effort, all good design will be universal.

Figure 19-2 Peterson project: The GE Living Center.

Figure 19-3 Peterson project: Pull-out work surface, with pull-out table and microwave-convection oven.

Figure 19-4 Peterson project: Induction cooktop area features smooth heatproof surface, sink and pull-out faucet adjacent to cooktop, and flexible storage and knee space below cooktop.

Figure 19-5   Peterson project: Computer center designed for flexible use.

Figure 19-6   Peterson project: Pantry or craft center designed for flexible use.

Figure 19-7 Peterson project: Island features seating, movable table, microwave at table height, and open storage.

Products and Sources

	Chapter 3. Aging in Place		
	Pictured product	**Manufacturer**	**Model line**
Figure 3-3	Ironing board hardware	Iron-A-Way, Inc.	
	Stacked washer/dryer	Whirlpool	
Figure 3-4	Shower door	Bel Pre Glass	
	Shower door handle		
	Grab bars	Broadway	
	Shower head	HansGrohe	
	Other shower fittings	Grohe	
	Corner shelf unit	Heath	
Figure 3-5	Bar sink	Kohler	
	Hot-water faucet	In-Sink-Erator	
	Under-counter refrigerator	SubZero	
	Microwave	GE	

	Chapter 4. A Vintage Home		
	Pictured product	**Manufacturer**	**Model line**
Figure 4-3	Refrigerator	SubZero	511
	Cooktop	Dacor	5GM362EM

Chapter 4. A Vintage Home (*Cont.*)

	Pictured product	Manufacturer	Model line
Figure 4-3	Sink	Elkay	SL41113
	Backsplash rail system	Hafele America	
	Faucet	Groeh	33-859
	Instant hot	Franke	
	Hood	Betlan Corp	Custom
	Microwave-convection oven	GE	JEB1090BV
	Counter	Soapstone	Custom
	Cabinetry	David Wothers	Custom
Figure 4-4	Sink	Kohler	K5986-2U
	Faucet	Groehe	33-859
	Dishwasher	Asko	1805
	Ovens	Gaggenau	EB184-610
	Counters	Soapstone	Custom
Figure 4-5	Custom work	David Wothers	
	Lighting	Arroyo	

Chapter 5. I Lost My Heart in San Francisco

	Pictured product	Manufacturer	Model line
Figure 5-3	Shallow sink	Elkay	
	Faucet	Delta	
	Cabinetry	Wood-Mode	
Figure 5-4	Shower/tub seat	Custom: Joseph Farais Studio	
	Grab bar in shower	Custom: Joseph Farais Studio	
	Mirror tilt-out brackets	Custom: Joseph Farais Studio	
	Lavatory wall supports	Custom: Joseph Farais Studio	
	Trap cover	Custom: Joseph Farais Studio	
	Bathroom cabinet	Flea market	

Chapter 7.   For Both of Us

	Pictured product	Manufacturer	Model line
Figure 7-3	Low-pile carpeting	Philadelphia	
	Bedding	Custom	
	Window treatment	Custom	
	Automated drapery control	Somfy Systems	
Figure 7-4	Sink	Kohler	Ladena

Chapter 8.   The Love of Life

	Pictured product	Manufacturer	Model line
Figure 8-5	Lavatory	Kohler	Invitation
	Lavatory single-lever faucet	Moen	
	Bathroom wall tile	American Olean	

Chapter 9.   Dreams Realized

	Pictured product	Manufacturer	Model line
Figure 9-4	Stair lift	Garaventa Ltd.	Stair-Lift

Chapter 10.   Mother and Child

	Pictured product	Manufacturer	Model line
Figure 10-3	Washer/dryer combo	Frigidaire	
	Vinyl flooring	Armstrong	
	Rolling cart	Custom	
	Secondary sink	Just	
	Faucet	Unknown	
Figure 10-4	Lavatory	Kohler	
	Toilet	Kolher	Wellworth
	Lavatory faucet	Moen	
Figure 10-5	Shower controls	Moen	

Chapter 10.   Mother and Child (*Cont.*)

	Pictured product	Manufacturer	Model line
Figure 10-5	Hand-held spray	Grohe	
	Floor tile	DalTile	
	Red grab bars	Linido	
	Ceiling-mounted supports	Linido	

Chapter 12.   On My Own

	Pictured product	Manufacturer	Model line
Figure 12-4	Sink	Kohler	Invitation
	Sink faucet	Kohler	Revival
Figure 12-5	Toilet	Kohler	Highline
	Grab bars	Pressalit	Fold Down
	Shower grab bars	Elcoma	
	Shower fittings	Grohe	
	Floor pavers	DalTile	
Figure 12-6	Nonslip tile	American Olean	Pavers

Chapter 13.   Freedom of Space and Spirit

	Pictured product	Manufacturer	Model line
Figure 13-3	Front door	Custom	
Figure 13-5	Tub	Jacuzzi	
	Tile mural	Custom: Jackie Smith, Gooseneck Designs	
	Grab Bars	GUSA—Ginger	Synchro
Figure 13-6	Toilet-bidet	Toto	Zoë
	Grab bars	GUSA—Ginger	Synchro
	Heater	NuTone	

Chapter 15. Real Life Design

	Pictured product	Manufacturer	Model line
Figure 15-2	Cabinetry	KraftMaid	
	Tile	Mannington	
	Floor	Armstrong	
Figure 15-3	Refrigerator	GE Profile	TPH21PRSBB
	Pull-out cutting board	KraftMaid	
Figure 15-4	Bifold hardware	Kiwi Connection	EZ Fold Hinge
Figure 15-5	Induction cooktop	GE Profile	JP692R
	Telescopic downdraft system	GE	JVB64S
Figure 15-6	Pull-out mixing bowl center	Custom	
	Pull-out table	Custom: KraftMaid	
	Secondary sink	Elkay Manufacturing Co.	
	Faucet	KWC	

Chapter 16. On the Street Where You Live

	Pictured product	Manufacturer	Model line
Figure 16-3	Telephone	GE	
	Cabinet pulls	SIRO	
	Door hinge and hardware	Hettich	
	Sink faucet	Grohe	
	Refrigerator	GE	
Figure 16-4	Toilet	Kohler	Highline
	Grab bars	HEWI, Inc.	
	Shower rods	HEWI, Inc.	
	Support arm	HEWI, Inc.	
	Towel rod	NuTone	
	Sink	Kohler	Chablis

Chapter 16. On the Street Where You Live (*Cont.*)

	Pictured product	Manufacturer	Model line
Figure 16-4	Faucet	Kohler	Finesees
	Lever handles	Kohler	
Figure 16-5	Medicine cabinets	NuTone	
	Grab bars	GUSA—Ginger	Synchro
	Multiposition support arm	Pressalit	

Chapter 17. Lifespan Design

	Pictured product	Manufacturer	Model line
Figure 17-2	Cabinetry	Heritage	
	Counter tiles	Marblex	
	Sinks	Kohler	
	Faucets	Jado	
Figure 17-3	Shower controls	American Standard	
	Hand-held spray	Groehe	
	Grab bars	GUSA—Ginger	

Chapter 19. The Living Center

	Pictured product	Manufacturer	Model line
Figure 19-2	Sink	Just Manufacturing Co.	Just Sink
	Sink motor	Accessible Design Adjustable Systems	
	Sink faucet	KWC Faucets, Inc.	
	Tile	Crossville	
	Cabinetry	Aristokraft Decora	
	Floor	Armstrong	
	Backsplash storage	Hafele America Co.	

Chapter 19.	The Living Center		
	Pictured product	**Manufacturer**	**Model line**
Figure 19-3	Microwave-convection oven	GE	JTP18BWBB
	Pull-out work surface	Hafele America Co.	
	Refrigerator	GE	TPX24BRYBB
Figure 19-4	Smooth cooktop	GE	JB660BVBB
	Island sink	Elkay Manufacturing Co.	
	Sink faucet	KWC Faucets, Inc.	
	Bifold hardware	Kiwi Connection	Ezyfold Hinges
Figure 19-5	Keyboard tray	Hafele America Co.	
	CPU wire basket	Hafele America Co.	
Figure 19-6	Stacked wire shelves and rolling cart	Intermetro Industries Corp.	
Figure 19-7	Microwave	GE	JEM25G

Manufacturers

**Accessible Design Adjustable
Systems (ACAS)**
94 North Columbus Road
Athens, OH 45701
(740) 593-5240

American Olean
1000 Cannon Ave.
Lansdale, PA 19446
(215) 855-1111
Fax: (215) 855-2252

American Standard
1 Centennial Ave.
Piscataway, NJ 08855
(732) 980-3150

Aristokraft Decora
1 Aristokraft Square
Jasper, IN 47547
(812) 634-2288

Armstrong World Industries, Inc.
P.O. Box 3001
Lancaster, PA 17604
(800) 233-3823

Arroyo Craftsman
4509 Little John St.
Baldwin Park, CA 91706
(626) 960-9411

Asko, Inc.
P.O. Box 851085
Richardson, TX 75085
(702) 833-3600

Bel Pre Glass
1050 1st St.
Rockville, MD 28050
(301) 982-0060

Betlan Corporation
3 Simm Lane
Newtown, CT 06470
(203) 270-7898

The Broadway Collection
250 N. Trost
Olathe, KS 66061
(800) 255-6365

Crossville Ceramics
P.O. Box 1168
Crossville, TN 38557
(931) 484-2110
Fax: (931) 484-8418

Dacor Appliances
950 S. Raymond Ave.
Pasadena, CA 91109
(800) 793-0093

DalTile
7834 Hawn Freeway
Dallas, TX 75217
(800) 933-TILE

Delta Faucets Co.
P.O. Box 40980
Indianapolis, IN 46280
(317) 848-1812

Elcoma
122 West Illinois St.
Chicago, IL 60610
(800) 621-1937

Elkay Manufacturing Co.
2222 Camden Ct.
Oak Brook, IL 60521
(630) 574-8484

Formica Corp.
10155 Reading Road
Cincinnati, OH 45241
(513) 786-3261
Fax: (513) 786-3024

Franke, Inc.
3050 Campus Drive, Suite 500
Hatfield, PA 19440
(800) 626-5771

Frigidaire Home Products
6000 Perimeter Drive
Dublin, OH 43017
(614) 792-4100
Fax: (614) 792-4073

Garaventa Ltd.
Box 1-1
Blaine, WA 98230

GE Appliances
Appliance Park
Louisville, KY 40225
(800) 626-2000

GUSA, Inc.
Ginger
250-S Executive Drive
Edgewood, NY 11717
(516) 254-0400

Gooseneck Design—Jackie Smith
2020 Hughes Shop Road
Westminster, MD 21158-2963
(410) 848-5663

Grohe America
241 Covington Drive
Bloomingdale, IL 60108
(630) 582-7711

Hafele America Co.
Box 4000
Archdale, NC 27263
(800) 334-1873

HansGrohe
1465 Ventura Drive
Cummings, GA 30130
(770) 844-7414

Samuel Heath
111 E. 39th St. STE 2R
New York, NY 10016
(212) 599-5177

Heritage Custom Kitchens
215 Diller Ave.
New Holland, PA 17557
(717) 354-4011
Fax: (717) 355-0169

Hettich America L.P.
6225 Shiloh Rd
Alpharetta, GA 30005
(800) 438-8424

HEWI, Inc.
2851 Old Tree Drive
Lancaster, PA 17603
(717) 293-1313
Fax: (717) 293-3270

In-Sink-Erator
Division of Emerson Electric Co.
4700 21st Street
Racine, WI 53406
(800) 558-5712

Inter Metro Industries Corp.
651 N. Washington St.
Wilkes-Barre, PA 18705
(570) 825-2741

Iron-A-Way, Inc.
220 W. Jackson St.
Morton IL, 61550
(309) 266-7232

Jacuzzi Whirlpool Bath
2121 N. California Blvd.
Suite 475
Walnut Creek, CA 94596
(800) 678-6889

Jado
7845 E. Paradise Lane
Scottsdale, AZ 85260
(800) 227-2734

Joseph Farais Studio
1905½ Adeline St.
Oakland CA 94607
(510) 268-3632
Fax: (510) 268-1144

Just Manufacturing Co.
9233 King St.
Franklin Park, IL 60131
(708) 678-5150

Kiwi Connection
82 Shelburne Center Road
Shelburne Falls, MA 01370
(413) 625-9506

Kohler Co.
444 Highland Drive
Kohler, WI 53044
(920) 457-4441

KraftMaid Cabinetry, Inc.
15535 S. State Ave.
P.O. Box 1055
Middlefield, OH 44062
(440) 632-5333

KWC Faucets, Inc.
1555 Oakbrook Drive #110
Norcross, GA 44062
(770) 248-1600
Fax: (770) 248-1608

Linido
3000 Xenium Lane North
Minneapolis, MN 55441
(800) 328-4058

Marblex, Design International, Inc.
2940 S. Prosperity Ave.
Fairfax, VA 72031
(703) 698-5595

Moen Inc.
25300 Al Moen Drive
North Olmsted, OH 44070
(800) 553-6636

NuTone
Madison & Red Bank Roads
Cincinnati, OH 45227
(800) 543-8687
Fax: (513) 527-5353

Philadelphia Carpet
c/o Shaw Industries
616 East Walnut Ave.
Dalton, GA 30721
(800) 241-9580

Porcelainite
20 Victor St.
Lexington, NC 27292
(336) 249-3931

Pressalit, Inc.
1259 Route 46, Building 2
Parsippany, NJ 07054
(800) 346-2380
Fax: (201) 263-8452

SIRO
6681 Bent Creek Drive
Rex, GA 30273
(770) 474-6688

Somfy Systems
47 Commerce Dr.
Cranbury, NJ 08512
(800) 227-6639

SubZero Freezer Co., Inc.
P.O. Box 44130
Madison, WI 53744
(608) 271-2233

Toto
135 East 65th St.
New York, NY 10021
(212) 288-7171

Whirlpool Corp.
Benton Harbor, MI 49022
(616) 923-5000

Wood-Mode, Inc.
1 Second St.
Kreamer, PA 17833
(717) 374-2711

Wothers, David (Custom Furniture)
246 School Alley
East Greenville, PA 18041
(215) 679-8928

Index

Aging, and household use, 5

American Association of Retired Persons (AARP), 5

American National Standards Institute (ANSI), 4

Americans with Disabilities Act (ADA) (1990), 4, 130
guidelines (1991), 4

Appliances, 32, 119–120, 141, 145, 169

Armoires, 61

Arthritis, 19, 143

Arts and Crafts style, 27, 31

Backsplash, 32, 144, 177

Banquettes, 33

Bath chairs, 42

Bathrooms, 10–12, 15, 19–22, 30, 42, 52, 60–61, 63–64, 71, 80–81, 88–91, 106–109, 119–120, 134, 156–157, 161, 163–164

Bathtubs, 12, 20, 42, 52, 63, 80, 108, 120, 163

Beall, Gordon, 15

Bedrooms, 15, 18–20, 22, 42, 51–52, 60–64, 71–72, 77, 81, 90, 97–98, 119, 121, 156–157, 163

Beds, 18–20, 52, 61–64, 98, 119

Bessler, John, 27

Bidets, 21, 63, 119

Bifold doors, 146

Blowers, 120

Bracht, Judith R., 161

Brain injuries, 67

Breashears, Bill, 70

Builder Magazine, 12

Bureaus, 20

Cabinets, 31–33, 42–43, 51, 90–91, 108, 119–120, 143–145, 163–164, 169, 177

California, house sale laws in, 67, 70

Ceilings, 31, 51, 90, 134

Center for Universal Design, 5, 8
  guidelines, 6–8

Cerebral palsy, 88

Chairs, 10–11, 42, 72, 119
  (*See also* Wheelchairs)

Chicago, housing guidelines in, 170

Civil Rights Act (1968), 4
  Fair Housing Amendment (1988), 4

Closets, 22, 33, 42, 61–63, 106–108, 119

Compartmentalization, 18–19

Computer stations, 81, 176–177

Convection ovens, 144

Cooktops, 32–33, 71, 143–146, 177

Corridors (*see* Hallways)

Corson, Bruce, 67, 70

Counters, 32–33, 41–42, 71, 108, 120, 143–145, 157, 169, 177–178

Decks, bathroom, 12, 20–21, 42, 63, 108

DeLaura, Jean, 167, 169–170

DeLaura Custom Builders, 167

Design (*see* Universal design)

Design One, 167

Dining rooms, 61–62, 71, 80

Disabilities, and household uses, 5

Dishwashers, 90–91, 143–144, 146

Dobkin, Irma Laufer, 15, 57, 103, 115, 153

Doors/doorways, 19, 21–22, 31, 50, 60–63, 71–72, 80, 89–91, 97–99, 106–107, 119, 121, 134, 146, 169

Dressing areas, 18–19, 21, 63, 163

Dust ruffles, 64

Elevators, 103, 121, 131, 134

Entries, 71, 80–81, 106, 118, 131, 133, 158

Equitable use, guidelines for, 6

Ergonomics, 11

Error tolerance, guidelines for, 7

Fair Housing Amendment (1988), 4

Faucets, 19, 33, 80, 134, 145–146

Faulkner, Winthrop, 129–131

Fire exits, 71

Fireplaces, 20, 119

Fischer, Chuck, 77, 80

Flexibility, 12

Flexibility in use, guidelines for, 6

Floor plans, 16–17, 28–29, 40, 48–49, 58–59, 68–69, 78–79, 86–87, 96, 104–105, 116–117, 132–133, 142, 154–155, 162, 167, 176

Floors, 31, 41–42, 50–51, 63, 80–81, 91, 97, 120, 145, 164, 178

Frank, Laurence A., 153

Freezers, 90–91

Furniture, assessment of, 10–11

Gardens, 71–72, 81, 89, 98–99, 119

General Electric, 141, 175

Grab bars, 12, 21, 42, 71, 90, 107, 119–120, 134, 164

Great rooms, 71–72

Grooming areas, 18–20

Guest rooms, 8, 98, 134

Hallways, 61–62, 71, 80, 98–99, 119, 156–157, 169

Headboards, 18, 20

Housing and Urban Development Department (HUD), 153, 156

Information, perceptible, guidelines for, 6–7

International Furnishings and Design Association (IFDA), 153

Intuitive/simple use, guidelines for, 6

Irion, Chris, 95

Jesse Owens project, 167, 170

Joseph P. Kennedy Institute for the Developmentally Challenged, 153

Kaplan, Ina Mae, 153

Kennedy Institute, 153

Kitchens, 10–11, 18–20, 30–33, 41–43, 51, 71, 80, 88–91, 97–98, 119, 141, 143–146, 157, 169, 175–178

Lassard, Chris, 47

Laundry areas/facilities, 21–22, 30–31, 33, 63, 90–91, 119–120, 176

Lebovich, William, 47, 57, 85, 103, 115

Libraries, 51, 81

Life expectancy, 5

Lifestyles, changing, 4–8

Lighting, 18, 20–21, 51, 70, 72, 89, 97, 119, 144–145, 164, 177–178

Linen closets, 62

Litz, Jane, 39

Living Center, 175–184

Living rooms, 80

Lohman, Mark, 77

Low physical effort, guidelines for, 7

Manufacturers, of products, 185–191 addresses, 193–197

McClure, Belinda, 115

McGrath, Norman, 131

Memory loss, 143, 146

Microwaves, 20, 30, 32, 91, 143–145, 177

Model lines, of products, 185–191

Moore, Charles, 39

Multiple sclerosis, 103, 109

Music rooms, 131

National Center for Health Statistics, 5

Neuberg, Carl, 161

Night tables, 20, 51

Noyes, Nick, 95, 97

Offices, home, 108–109

Ovens, 32, 89, 143–146, 175

Pantries, 30–31, 33, 42, 71, 144, 169

Peabody & Stearns, 27

Perceptible information, guidelines for, 6–7

Peterson, Mary Jo, 10, 27, 85, 141, 175

Physical effort, low, guidelines for, 7

Polk, David, 27

Pools, 30, 81, 98, 107

Principles of Universal Design, 5–8

Private homes, sample projects from, 15–125, 131–184

Products (*see* Manufacturers)

Programs, design process, 9–12

Public standards, 4

Quadriplegics, 77, 88

Rails, 12, 71, 169

Ralston-Latham, Donna, 153

Ramps, 41, 43, 60, 80–81, 158, 169

Ray, Geary, 70

Real Life Design Kitchen, 141–151, 175

Reception galleries, 131, 134

Refrigerators, 20, 32, 81, 88, 90, 143–144, 177

Rolling carts, 144–146

Rooms, and household uses, 4–5

Ryder, Tom, 67

Scooters, 106, 108

Shower chairs, 90–91

Showerheads, 120, 164

Showers, 11–12, 20–21, 61, 63, 71, 80, 90–91, 107–109, 120, 134, 163–164

Simple/intuitive use, guidelines for, 6

Sinks, 11, 18, 32–33, 41–42, 61, 71, 80–81, 90–91, 106–108, 120, 134, 143–144, 146, 157, 163–164, 176–177

Size/space for use, guidelines for, 7

Skylights, 21, 41, 89

Sound problems, 18

Space/size for use, guidelines for, 7

Sprains, 115

Stairlifts, 81

Standards, public, 4

Stewart, Craig, 115

Stoves, 32–33, 41, 71, 89, 143–146, 177

Tables, 20, 32–33, 51, 88, 90–91, 119, 144–145, 163, 176–177

Televisions, 18, 20, 51, 62, 119

Theaters, home, 51

Thompson, Boyce, 12

Toaster ovens, 91

Toilets, 12, 21, 61, 63, 71, 80, 90,
    106–107, 119–120, 134, 163
Tolerance for error, guidelines for,
    7
Tradition, 12
Transfer surfaces, 32–33, 41–42, 90,
    114
Trapeze grips, 90

Uniform Federal Accessibility Stan-
    dard (UFAS), 4
Universal design, 129–130
  and changing lifestyles, 4–8
  defined, 3
  guidelines for, 6–8
  process, 9–12
  and public standards, 4
Utility rooms, 81

Virginia Technical Institute, 146
Vision loss, 143, 146

Walkers, 20
Walkways, 118–119, 121, 131, 158
Wallis, E. J., 67
Wheelchairs, 20–21, 30, 42, 47,
    50–52, 57, 60–63, 70–71, 88,
    90–91, 106, 120, 131, 157
Whirlpools, 63, 120
Windows, 20, 31, 33, 41–42, 62, 71,
    89, 98, 144
Work surfaces, 32, 42, 143–145,
    175–178
Wright, Frank Lloyd, 129

Ziegler, R. Dale, 85
Zoë toilet, 119

About the Authors

Irma Dobkin is an award-winning interior and space designer who has run her own design firm, Irma Dobkin Interiors, Ltd., in Bethesda, MD, since 1986. The recipient of the ASID Design for Humanity Award in 1995, she has written a number of notable professional papers and designed and conducted numerous professional seminars.

Mary Jo Peterson is a nationally recognized, award-winning expert, consultant, and speaker on universal kitchen and bath design. She has consulted with such companies as GE Appliances, USHomes, and Del Webb on home and product design, and has provided design services for hundreds of architects, homebuilders, and homeowners. She has spoken before a number of national professional design organizations. For the National Kitchen and Bath Association, she conducts a regularly scheduled seminar on universal design. Her firm, Mary Jo Peterson, Inc., Design Consultants, is based in Brookfield, CT.